COPYRIGHT © 2018

ALL RIGHTS RESERVED.
NO PART OF THIS PUBLICATION
MAY BE REPRODUCED,
DISTRIBUTED, OR TRANSMITTED
IN ANY FORM OR BY ANY MEANS,
INCLUDING PHOTOCOPYING,
RECORDING, OR OTHER
ELECTRONIC OR MECHANICAL
METHODS, WITHOUT
THE PRIOR WRITTEN
PERMISSION OF THE PUBLISHER,
EXCEPT IN THE CASE OF BRIEF
QUOTATIONS EMBODIED
IN CRITICAL REVIEWS
AND CERTAIN OTHER
NONCOMMERCIAL USES
PERMITTED BY COPYRIGHT LAW.

Retirement Coloring Book

THIS BOOK
BELONGS TO

_____

_____

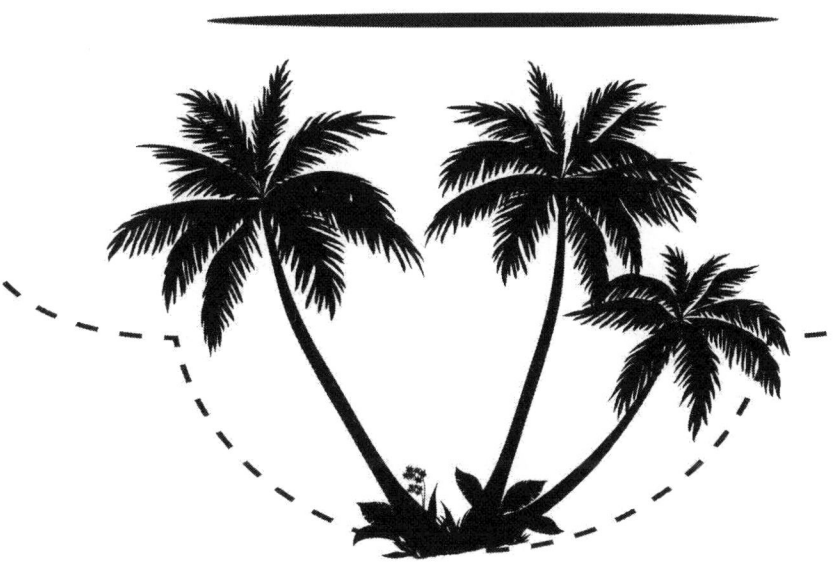

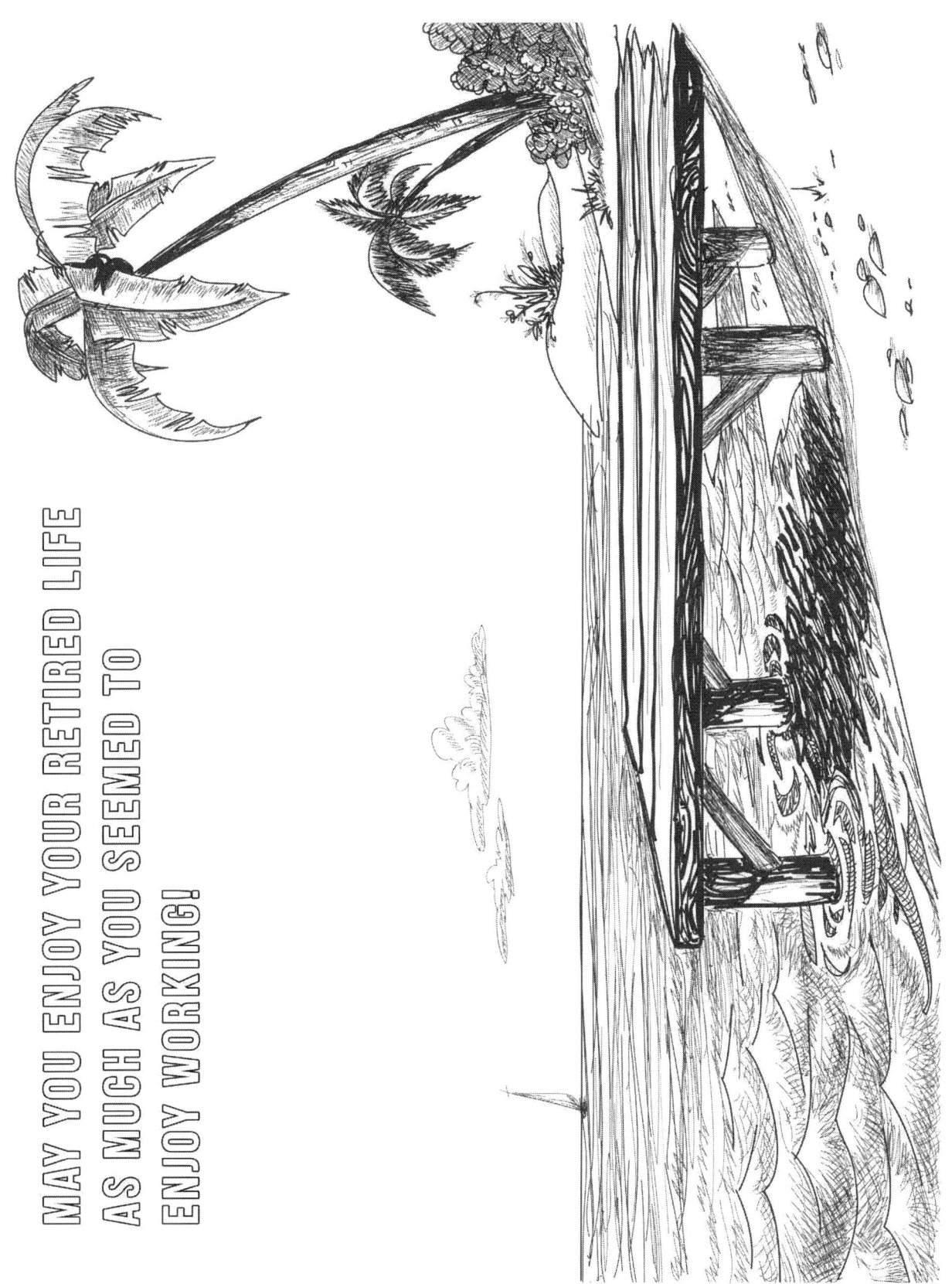

MAY YOU ENJOY YOUR RETIRED LIFE AS MUCH AS YOU SEEMED TO ENJOY WORKING!

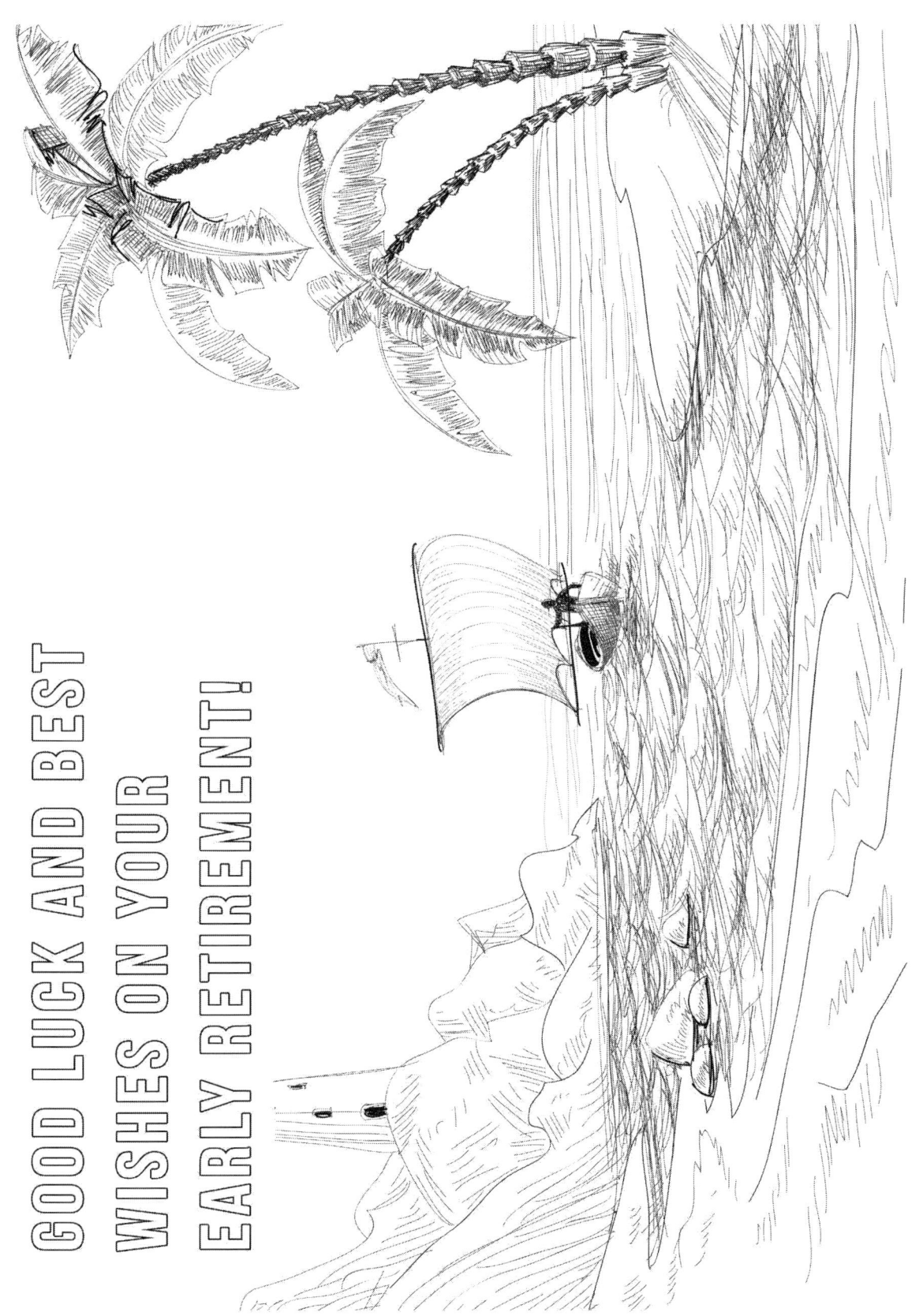

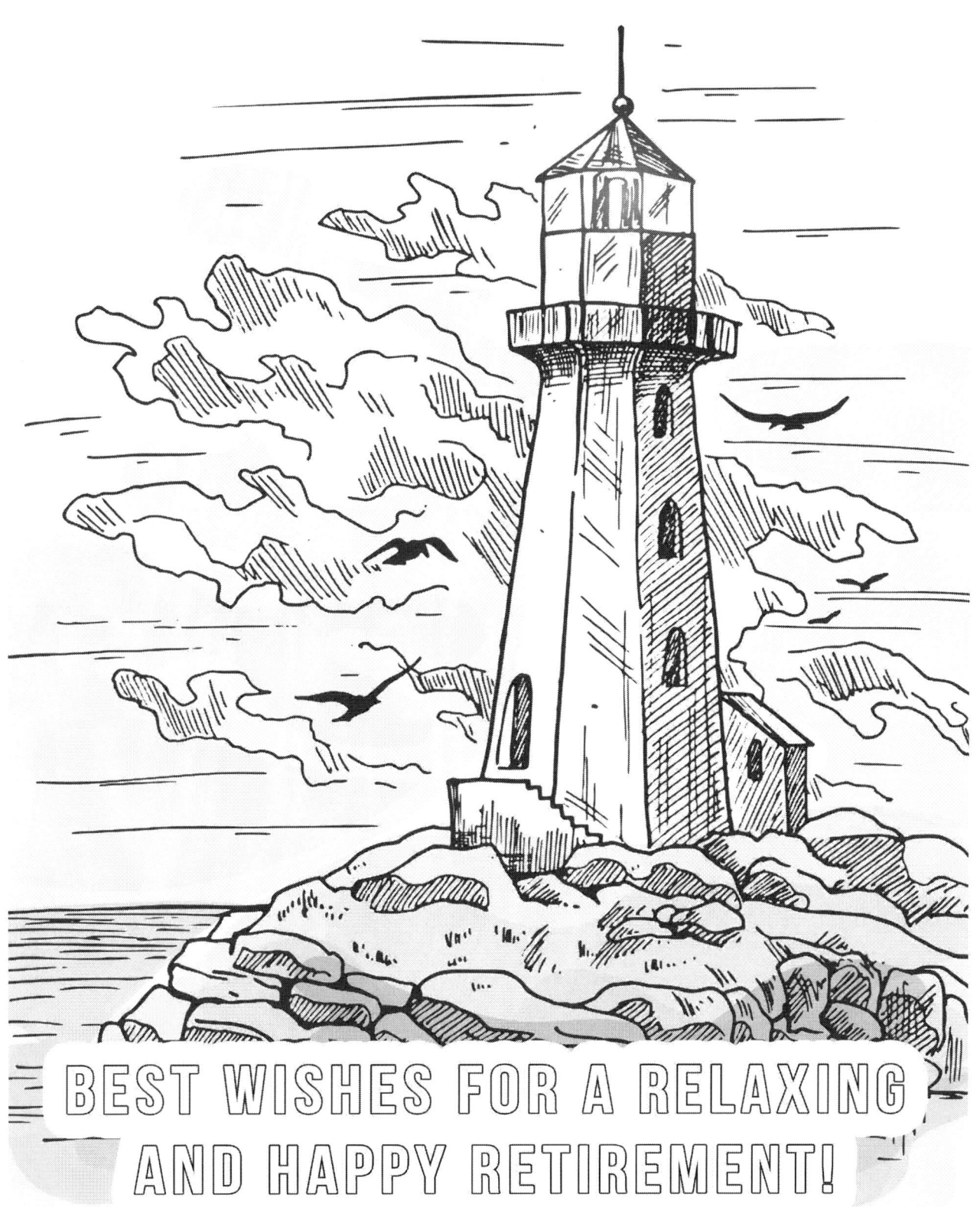

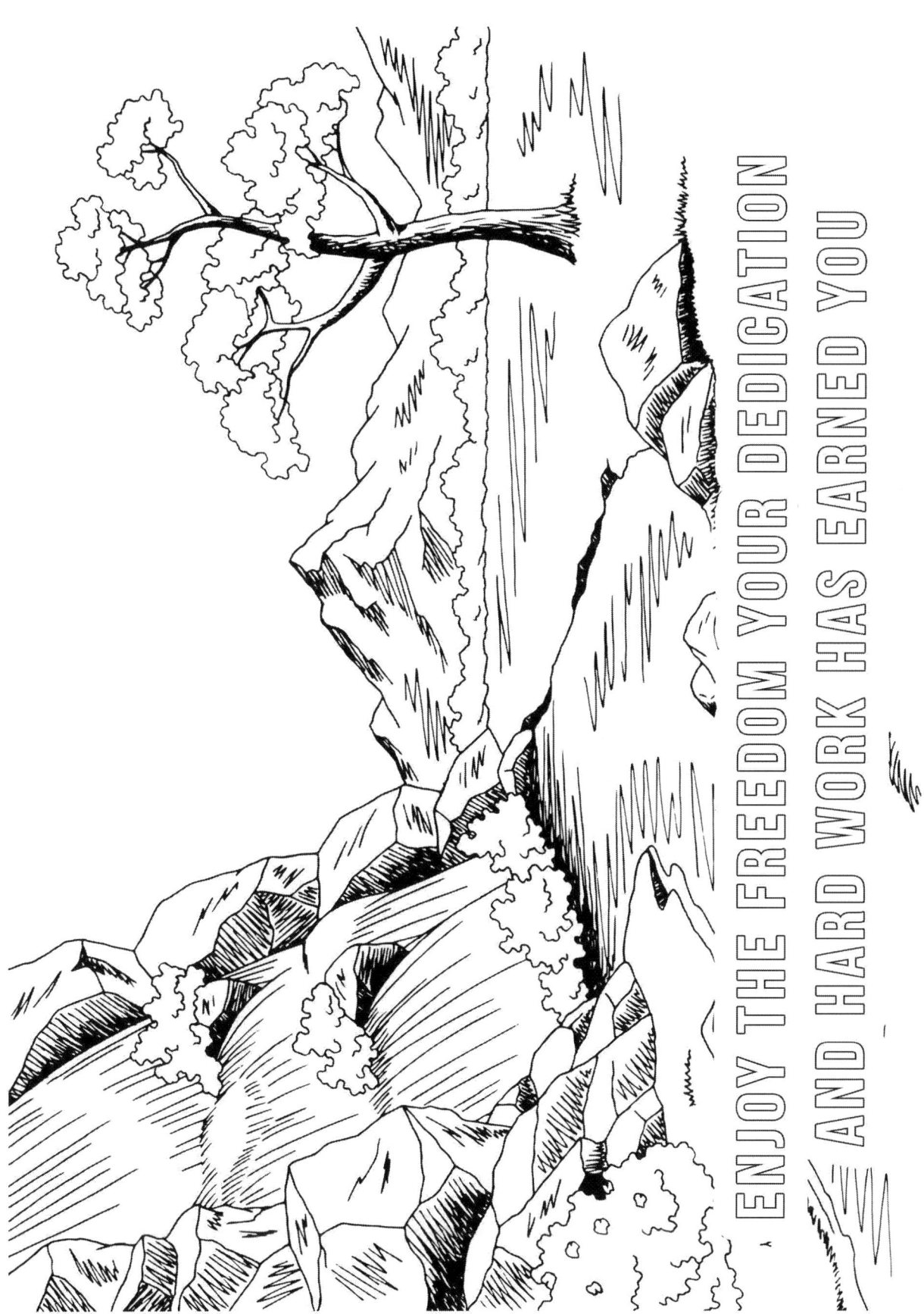

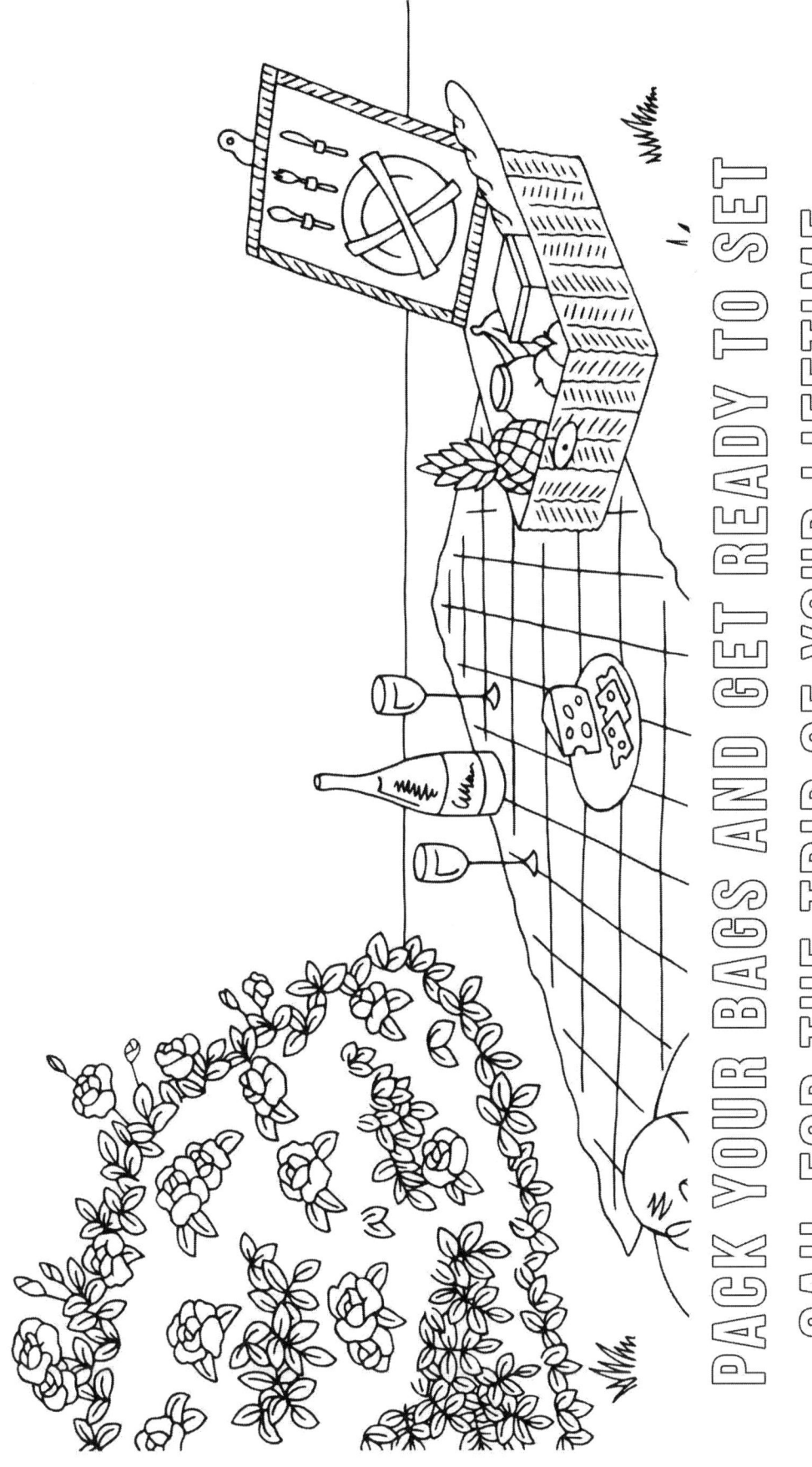

PACK YOUR BAGS AND GET READY TO SET SAIL FOR THE TRIP OF YOUR LIFETIME.

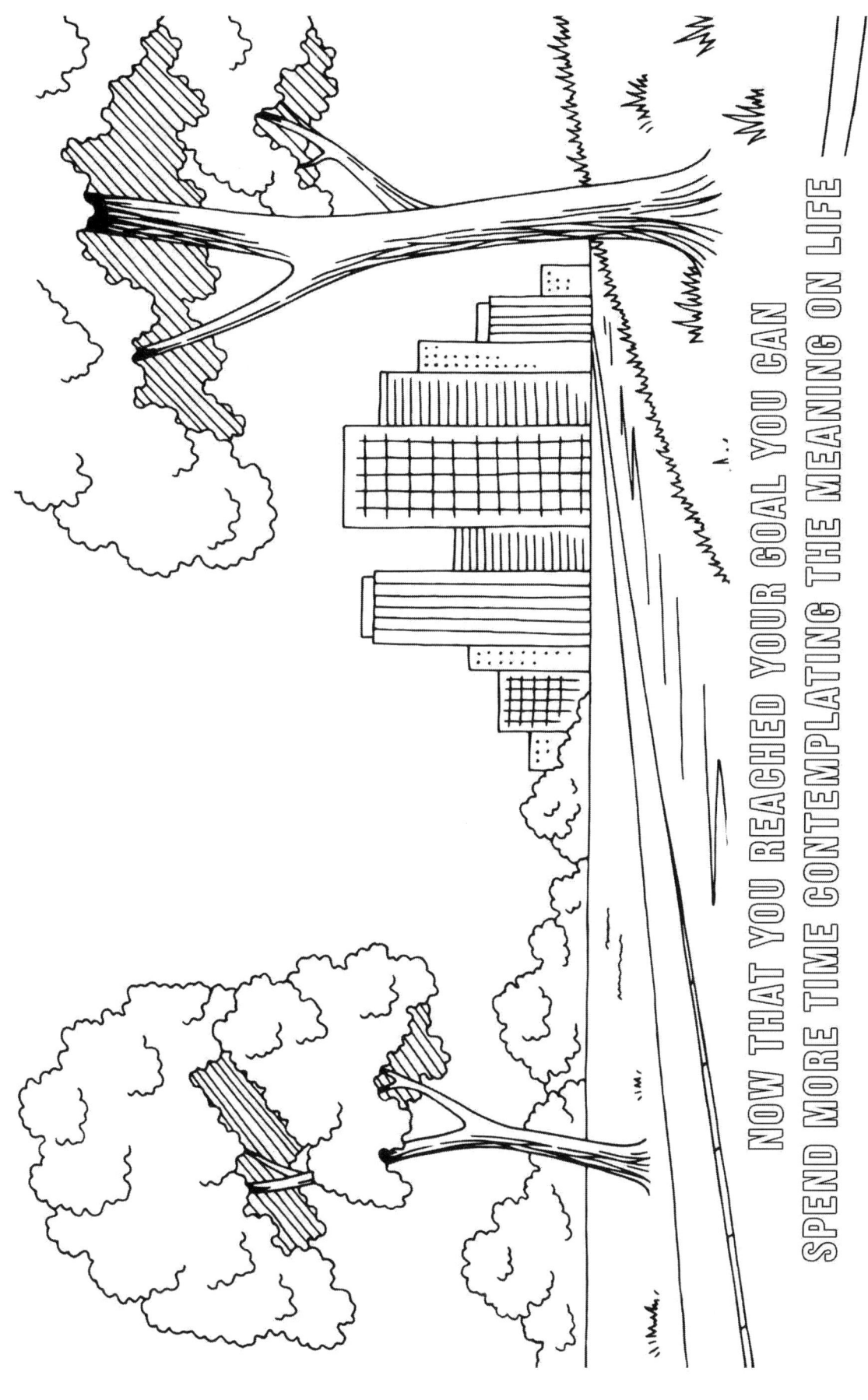

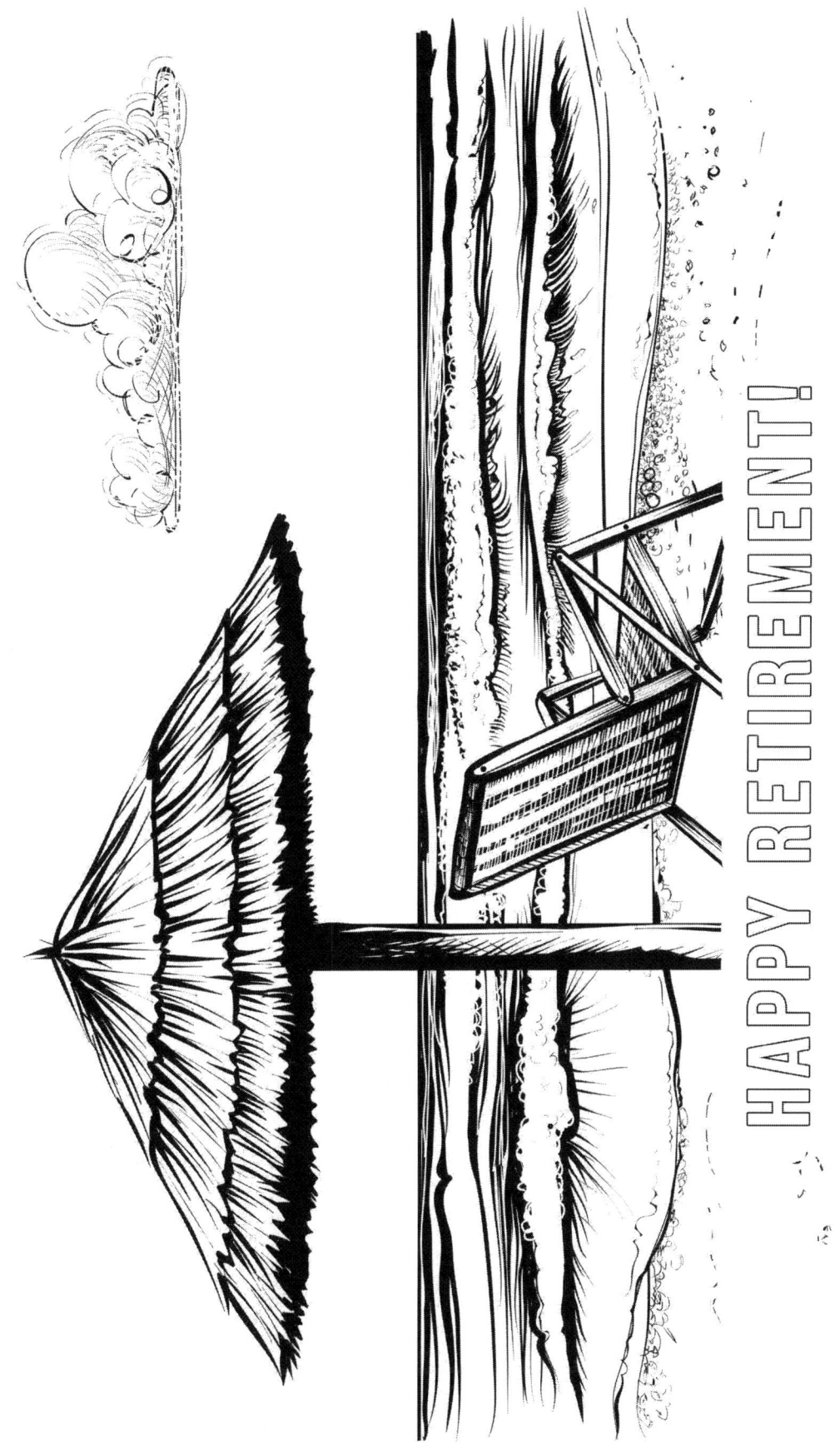

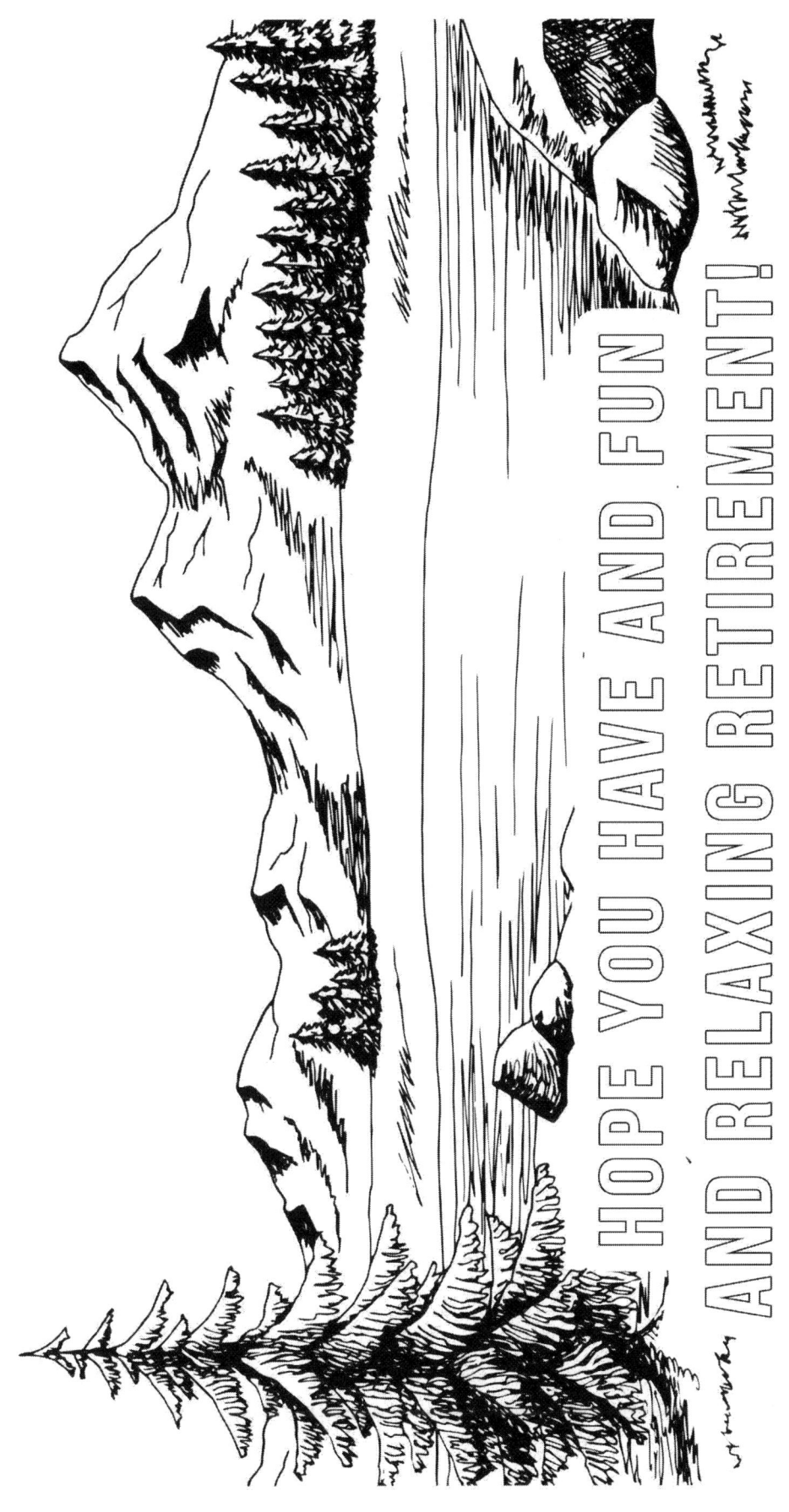

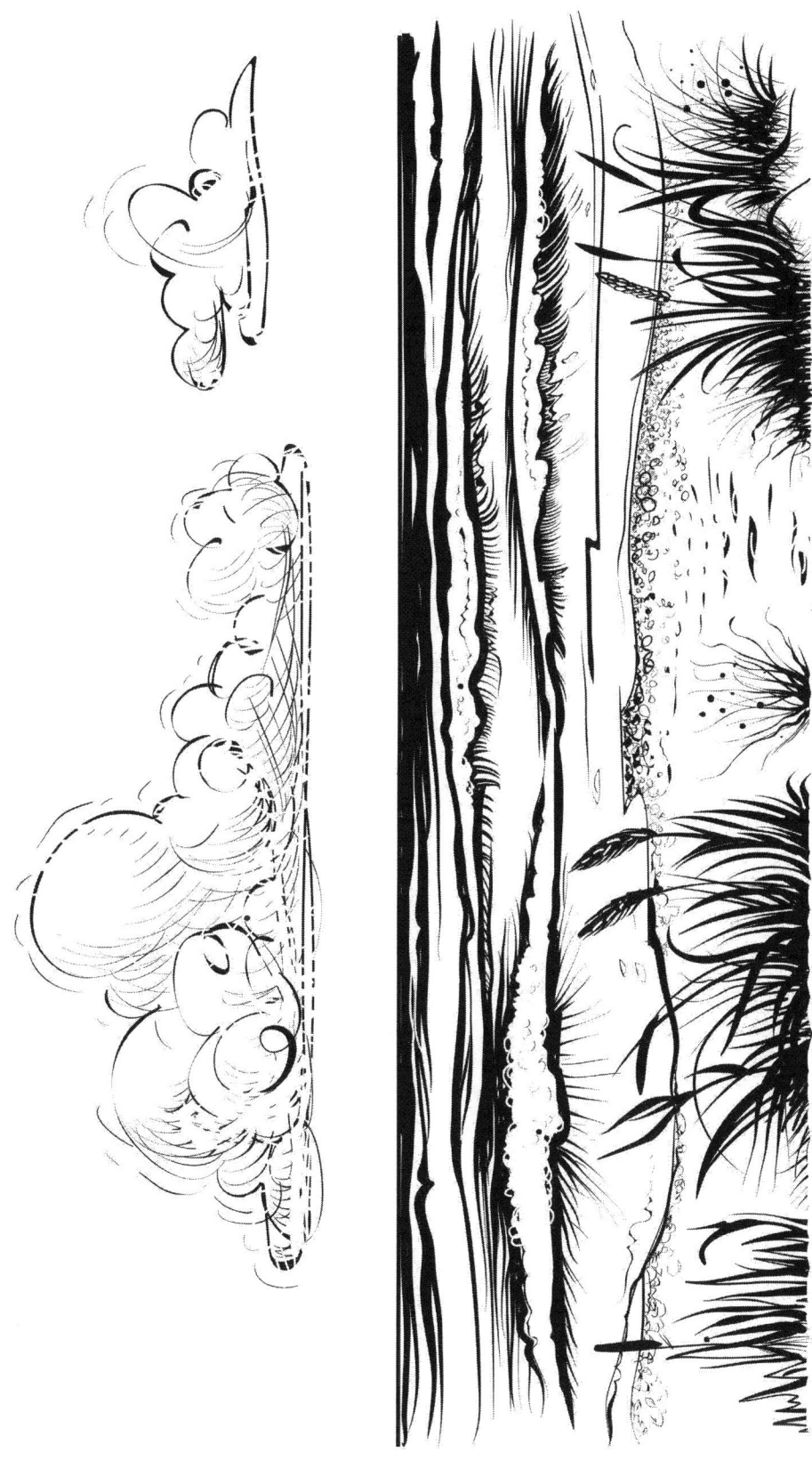

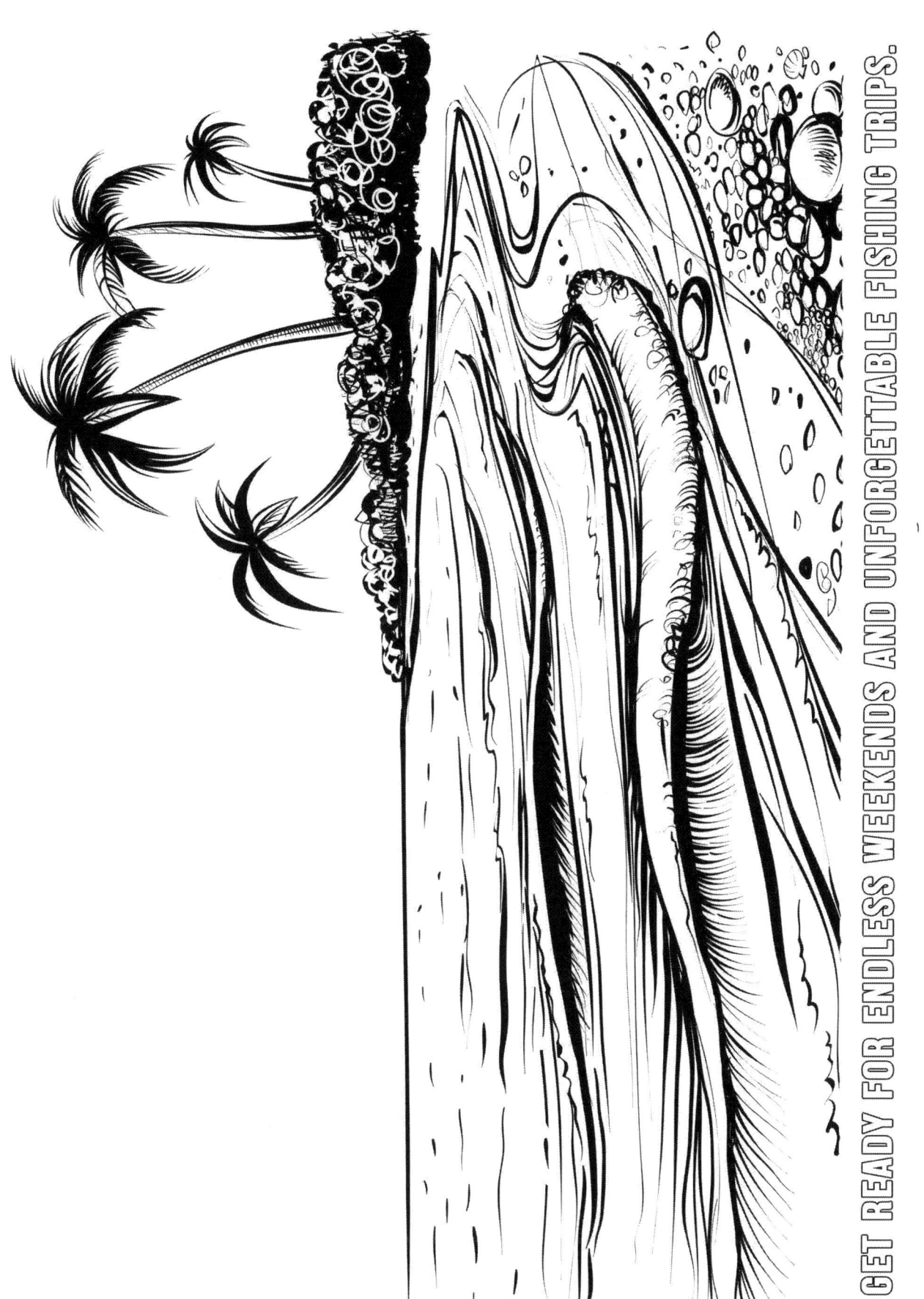

CONGRATULATIONS ON YOUR RETIREMENT!

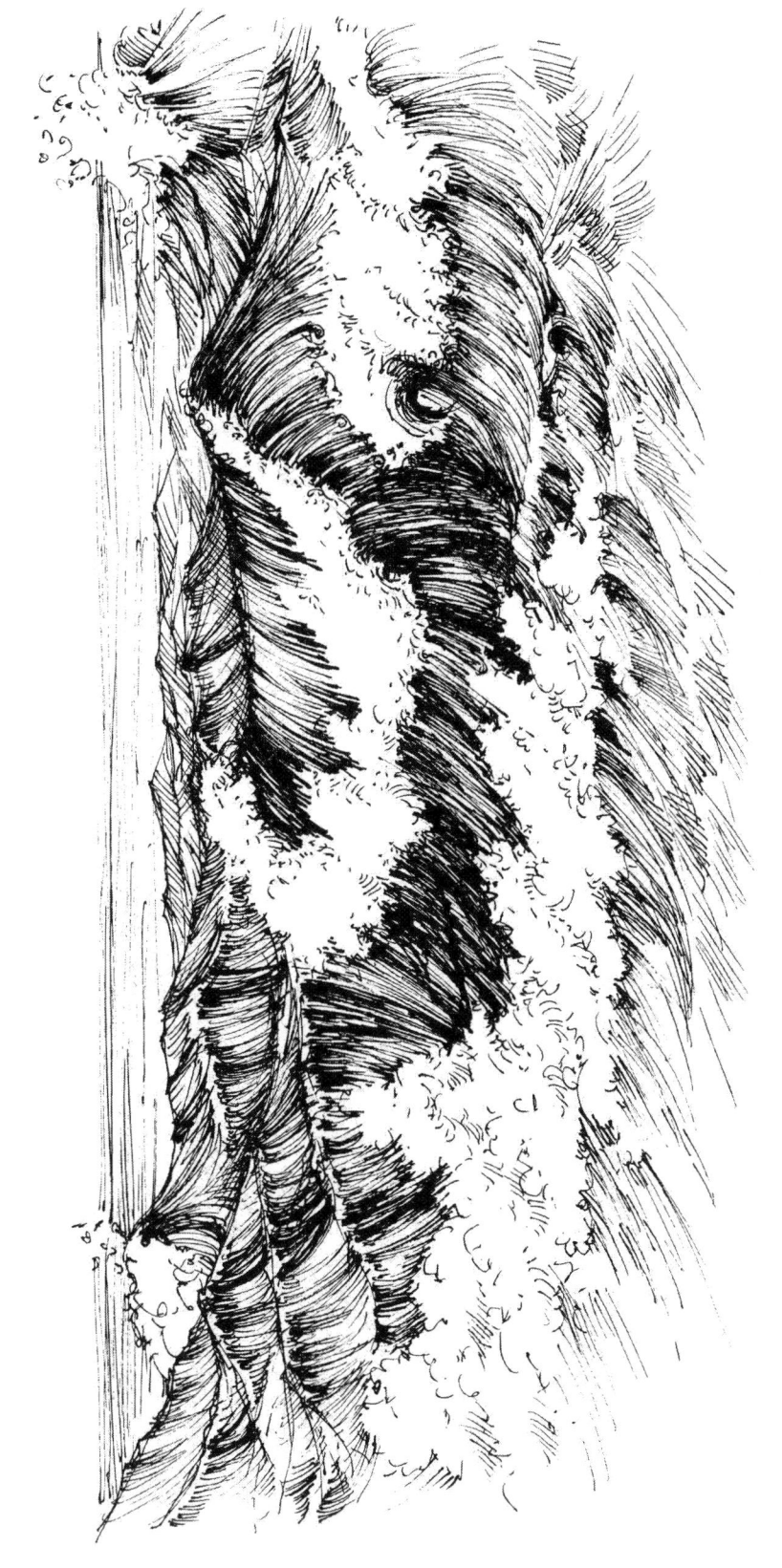

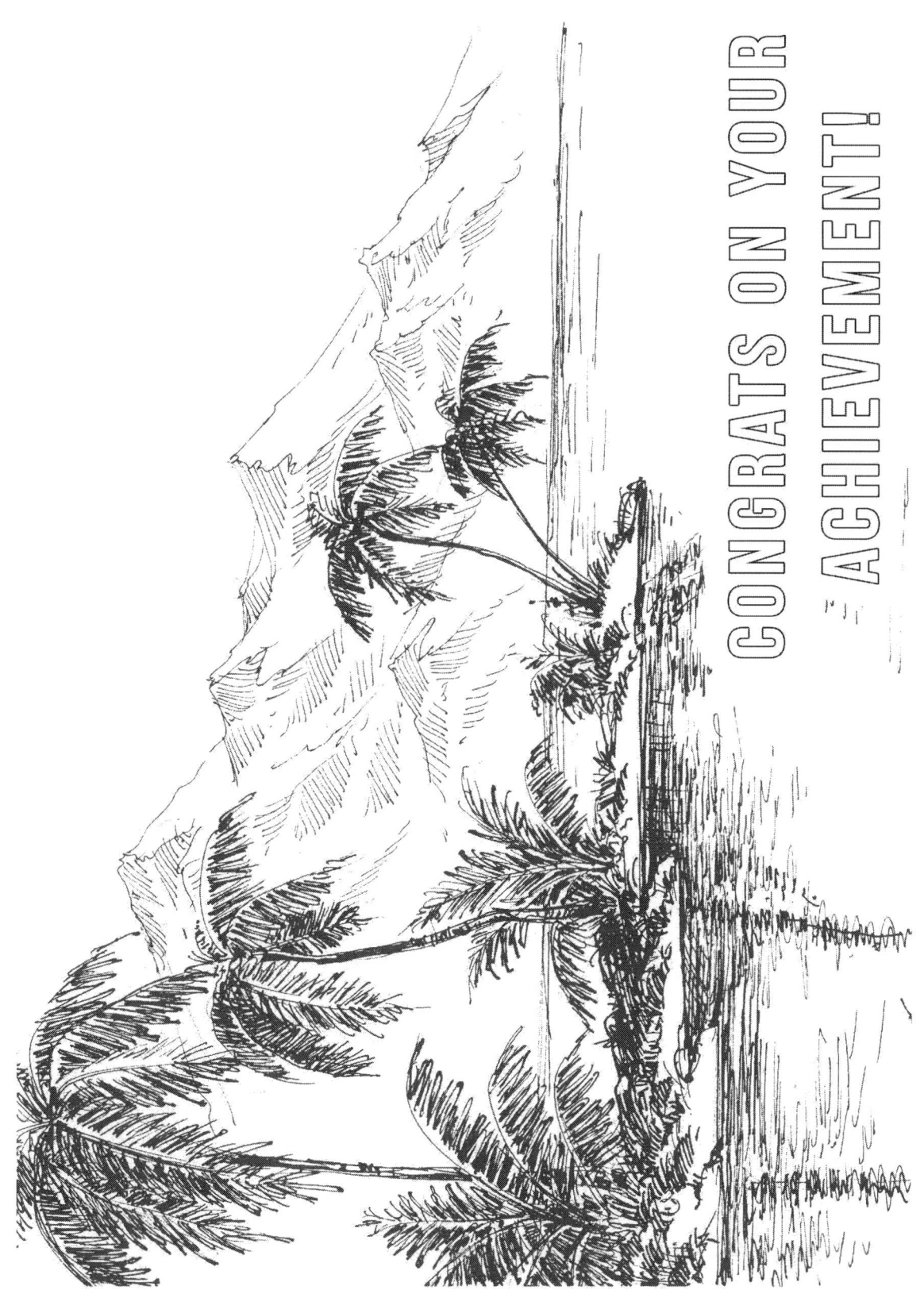

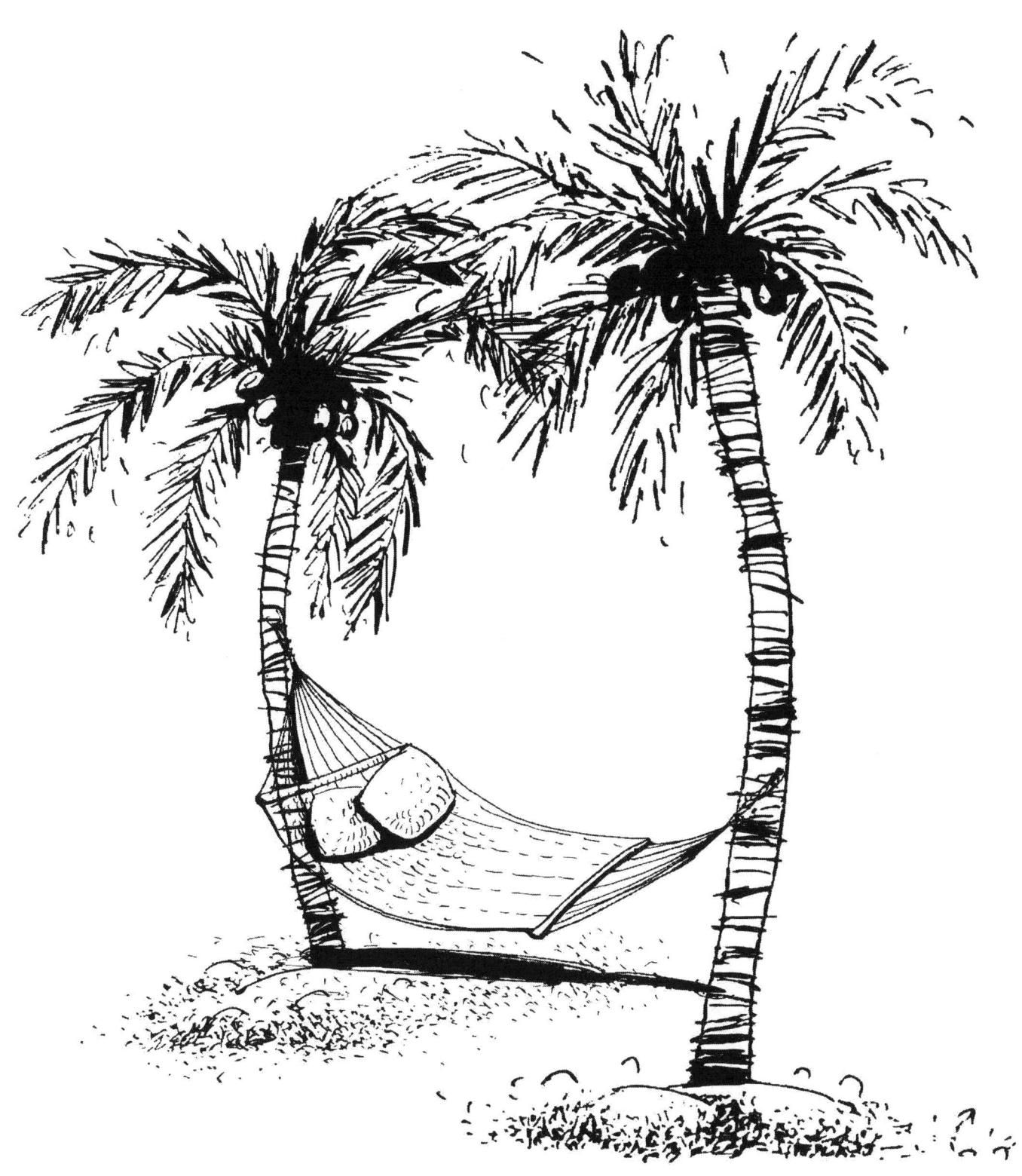

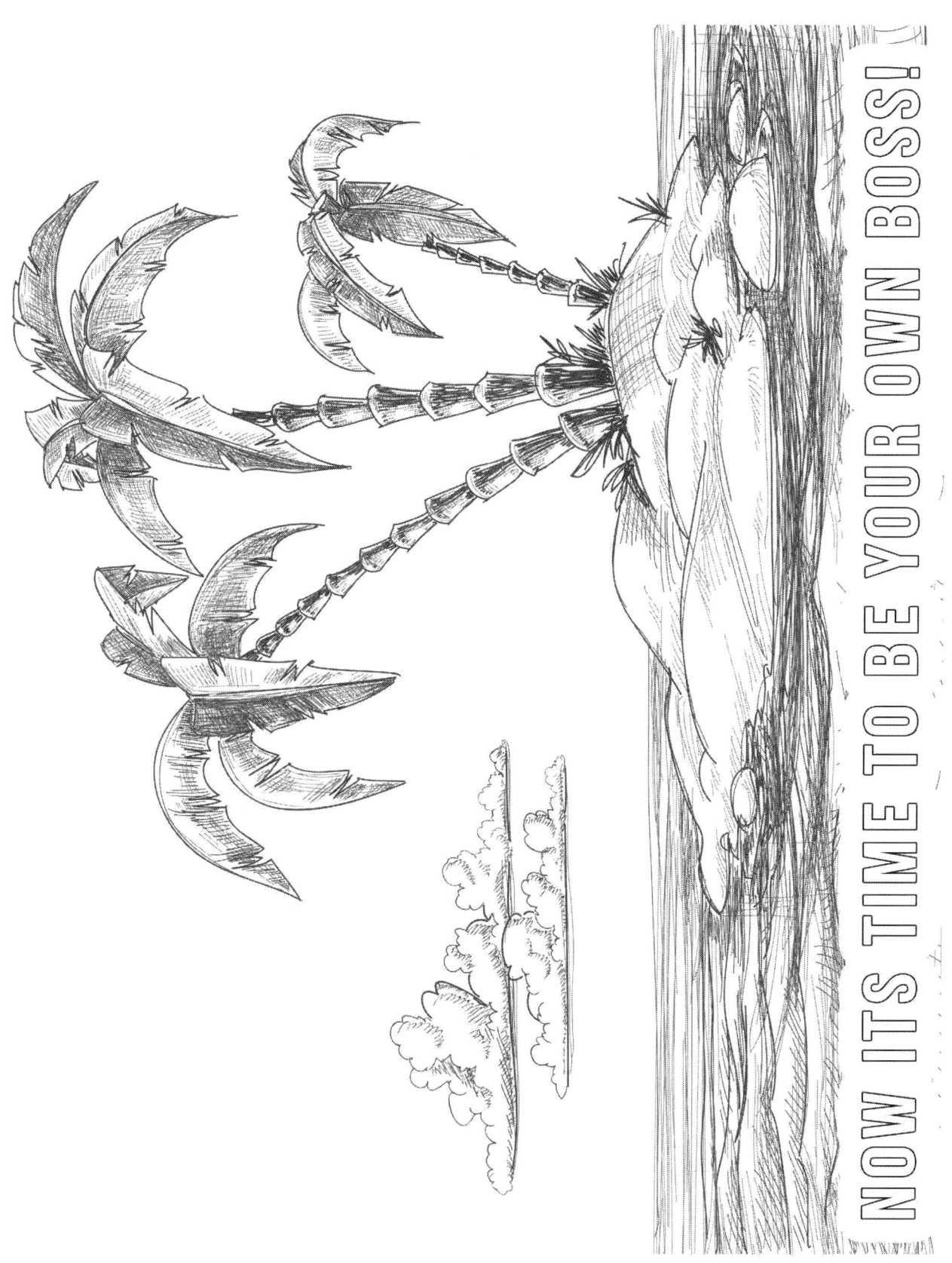

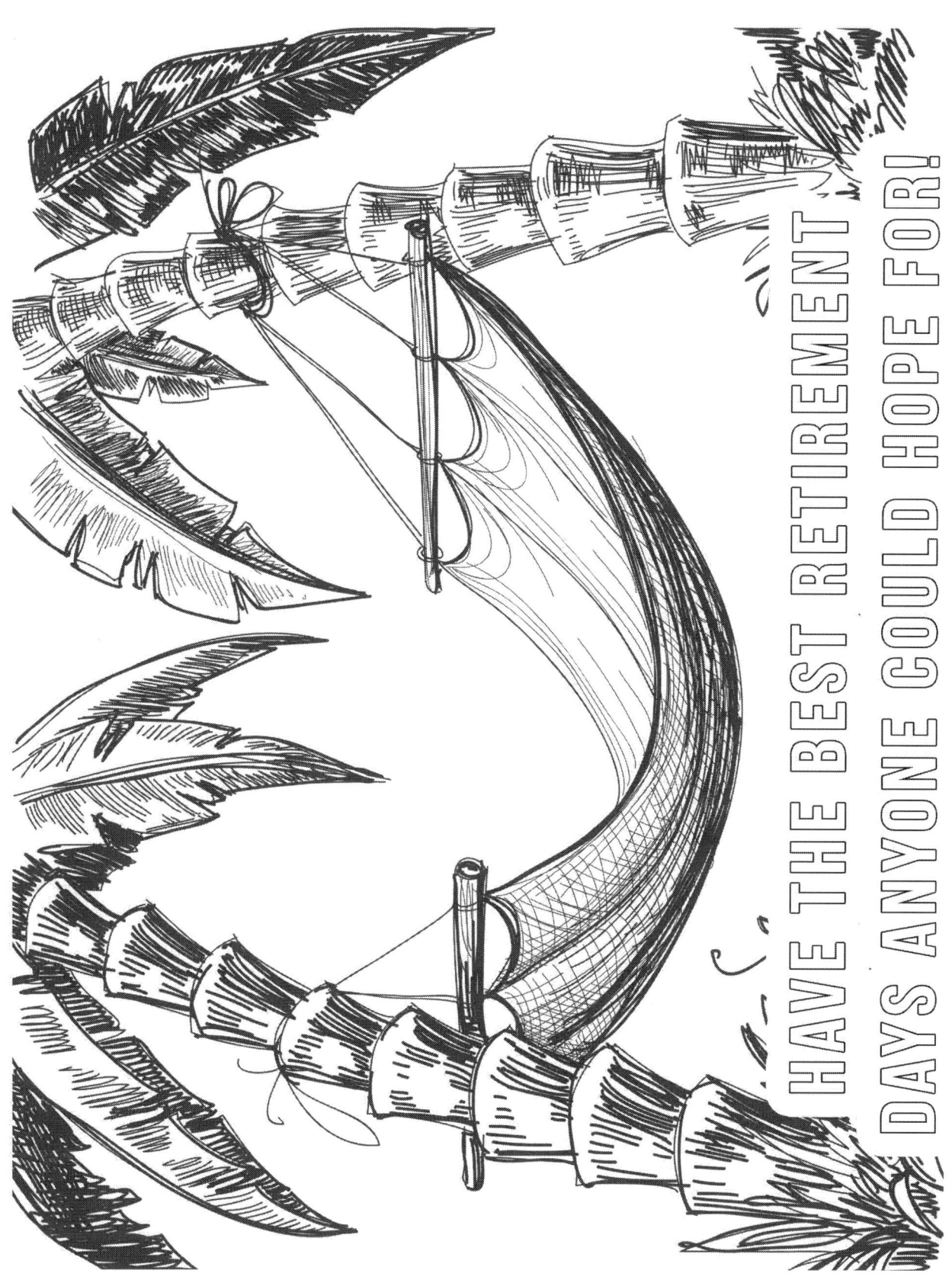

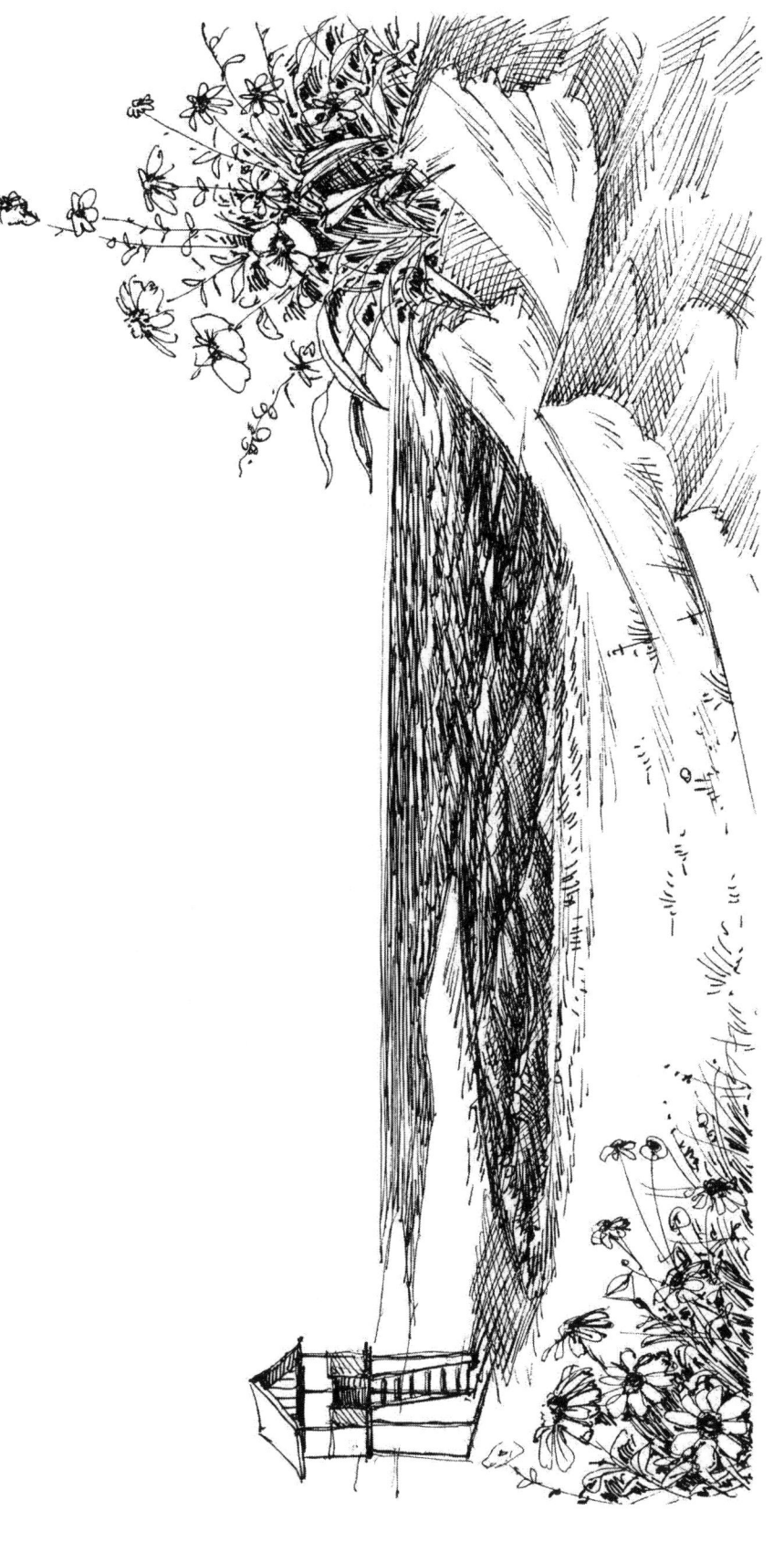

YOU'VE SUCEEDED IN YOUR CAREER, NOW ITS TIME TO SUCEED IN RETIREMENT!

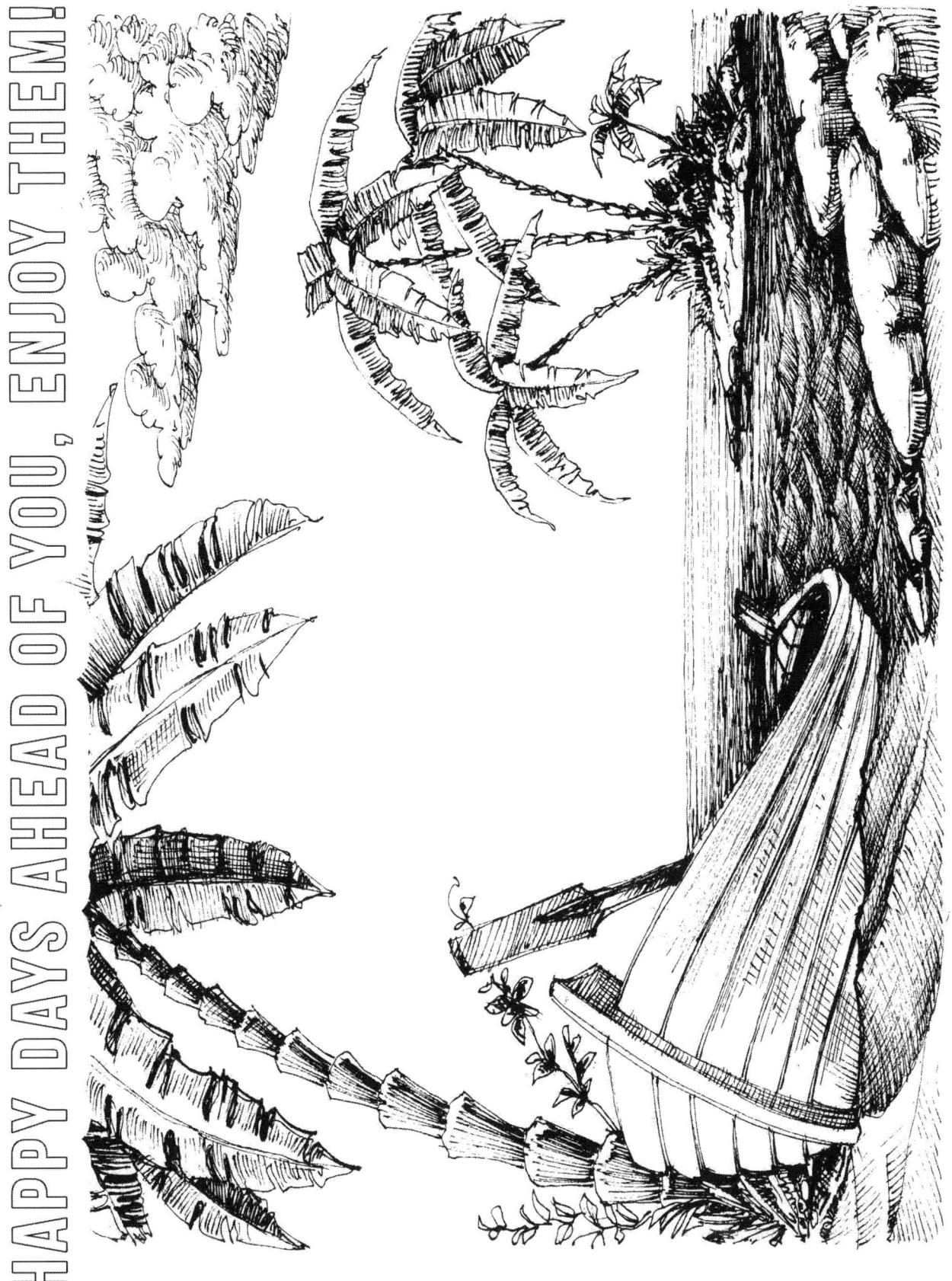

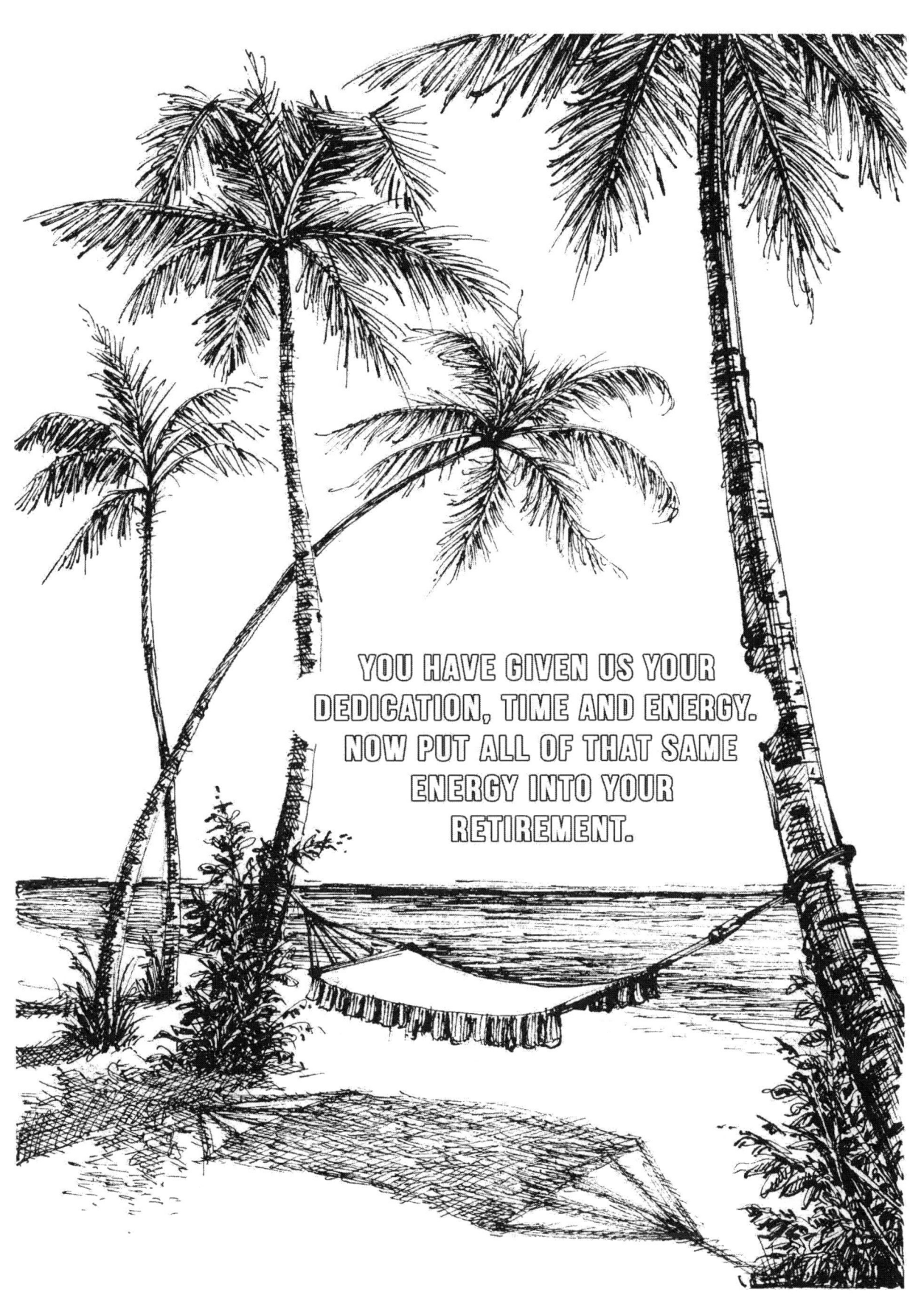

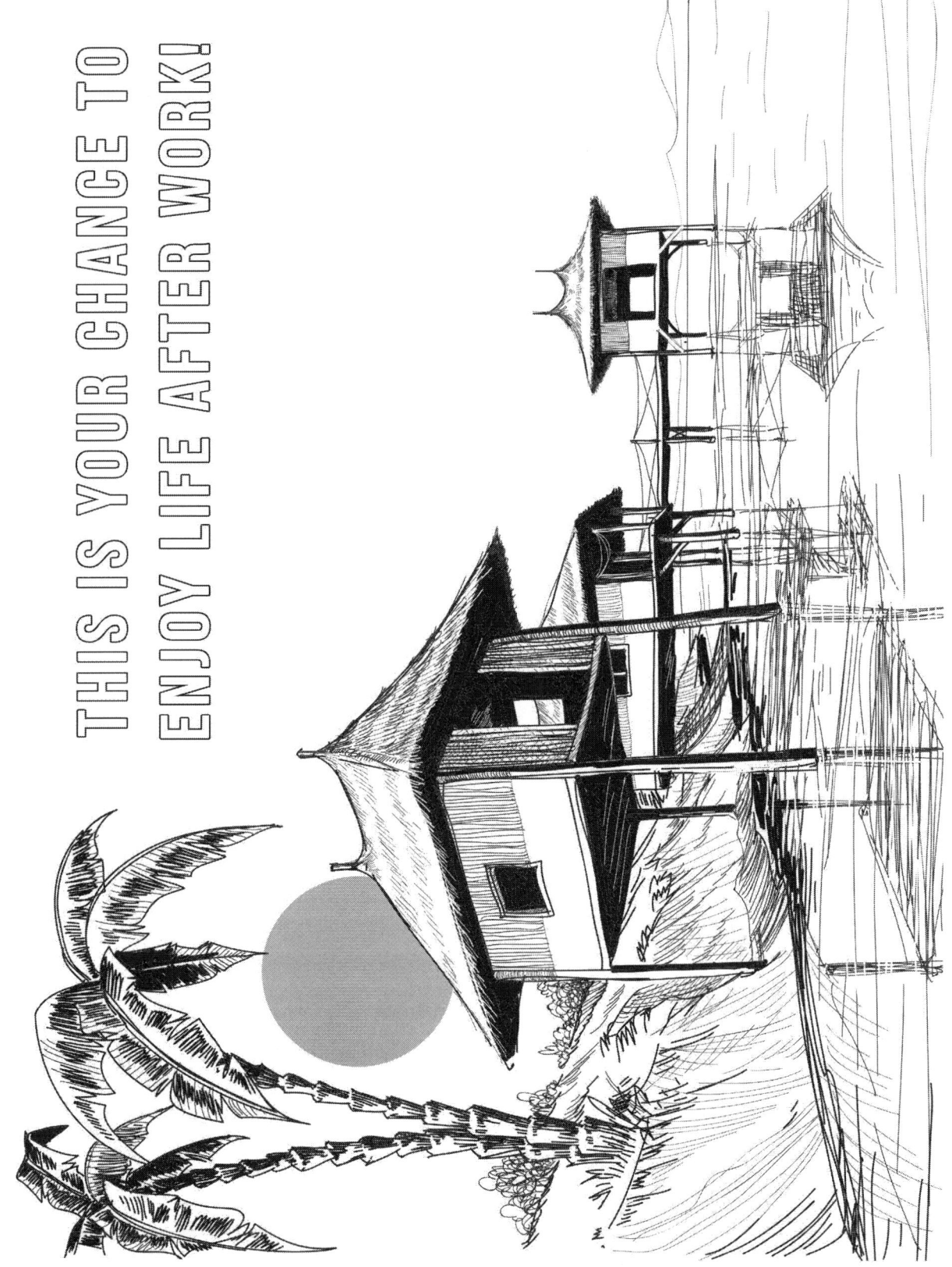

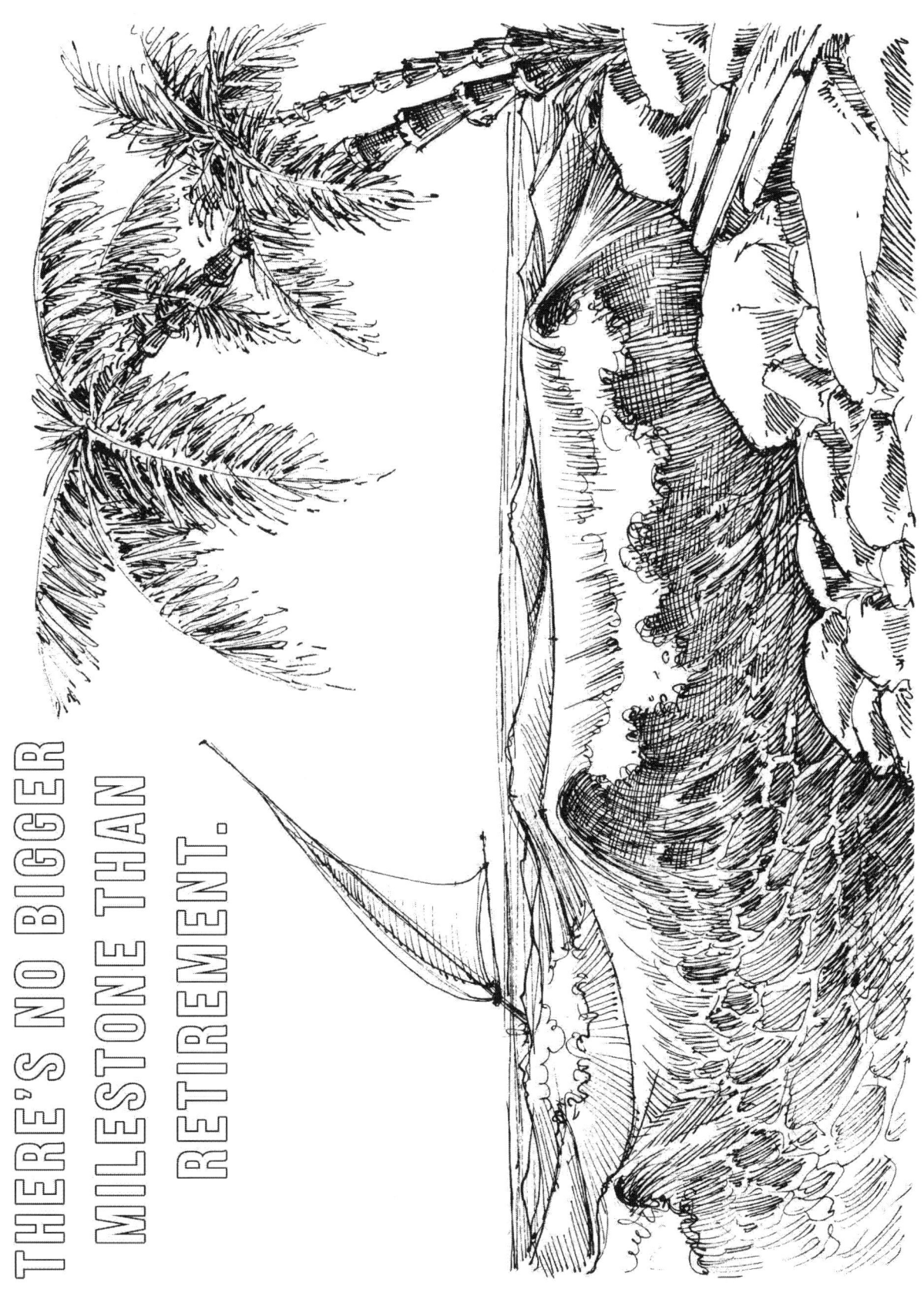

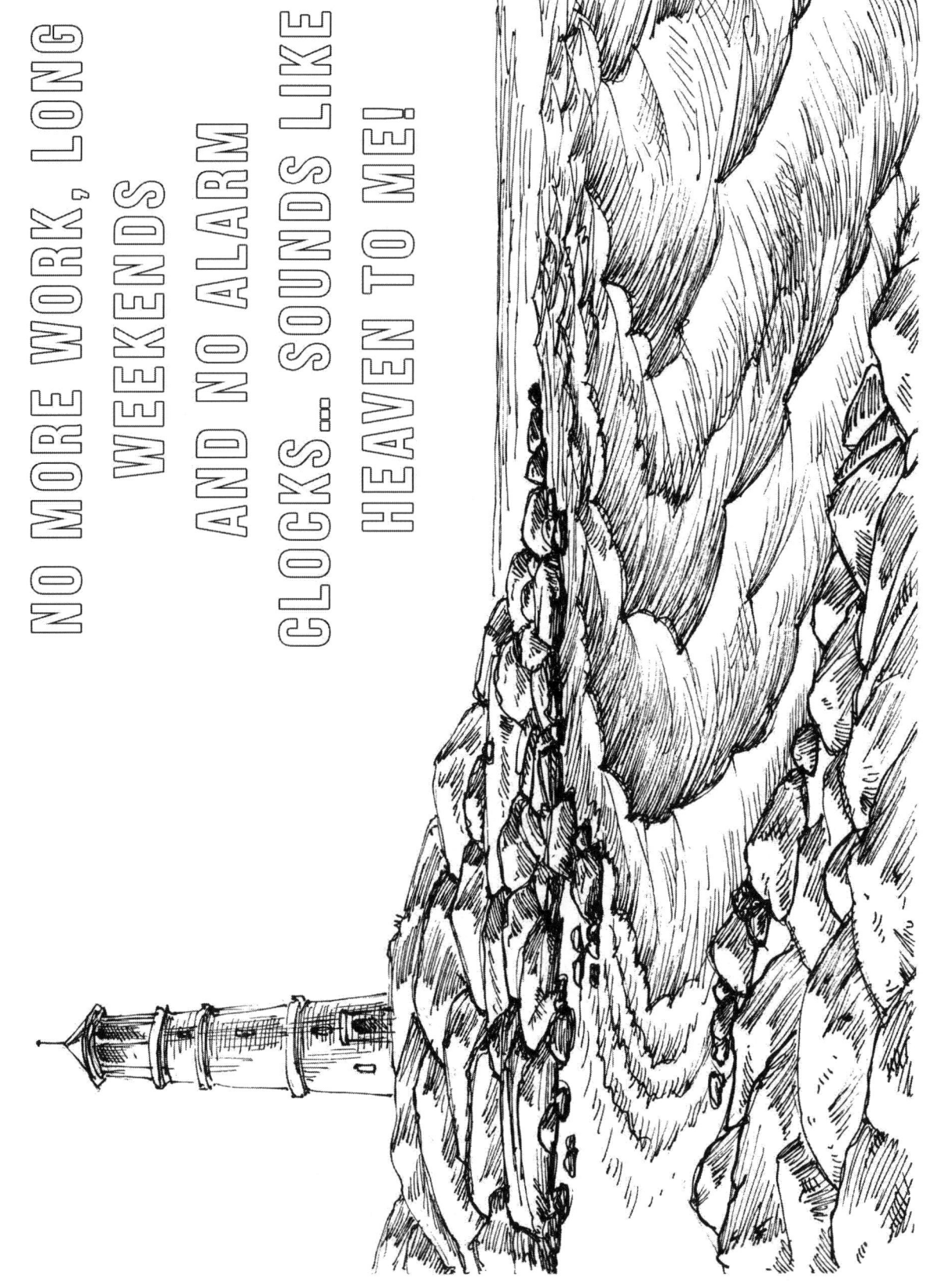

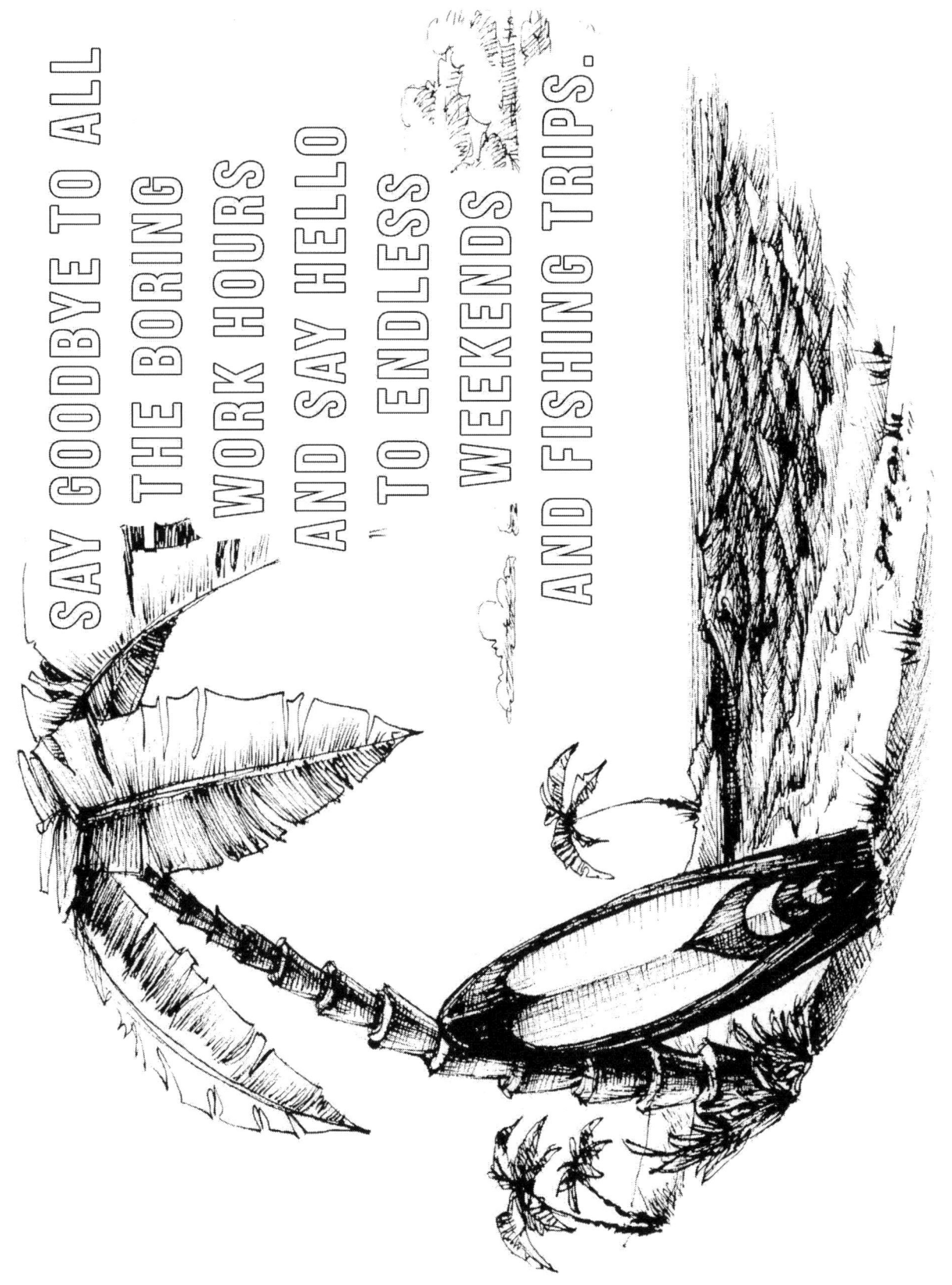

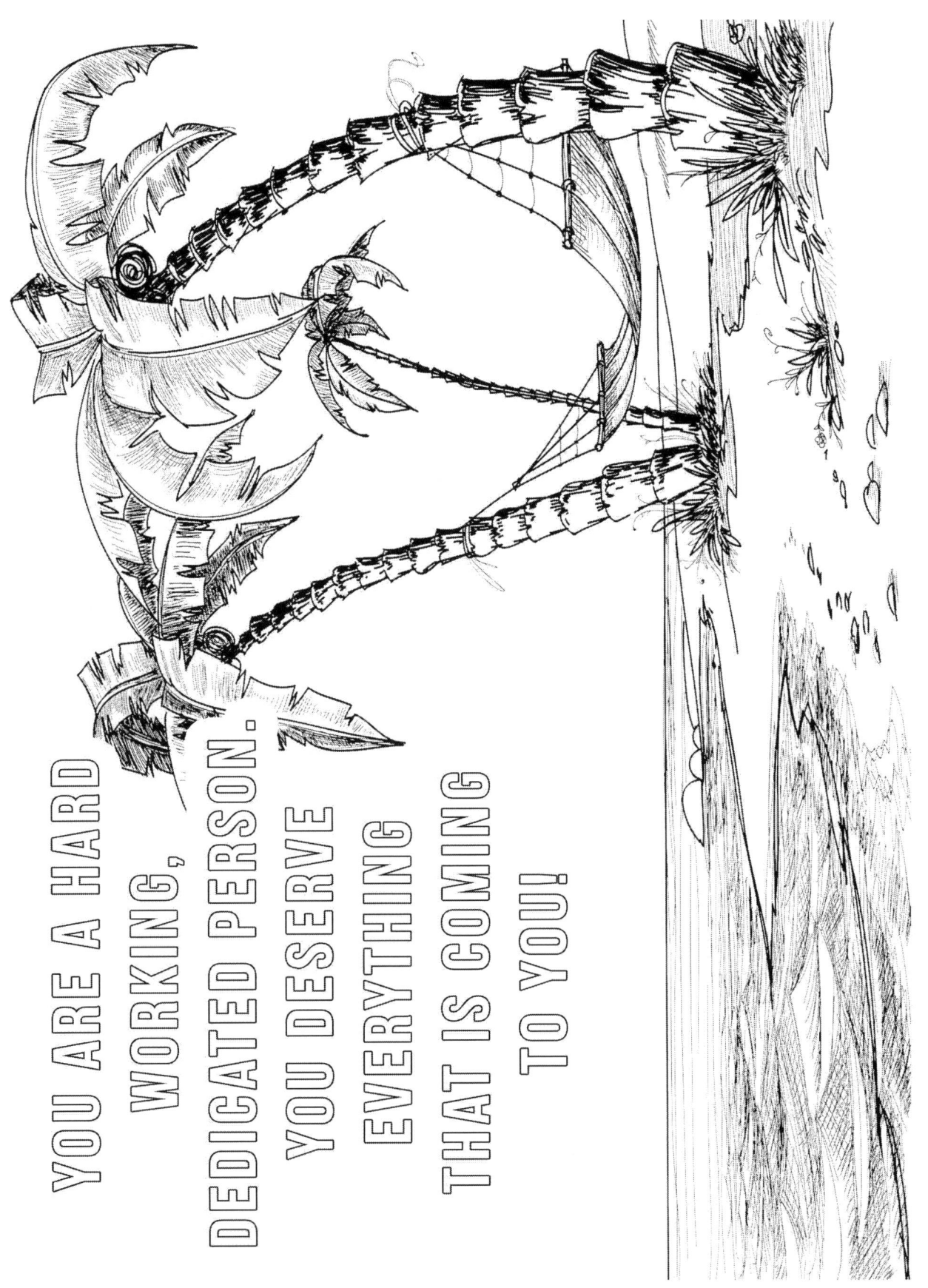

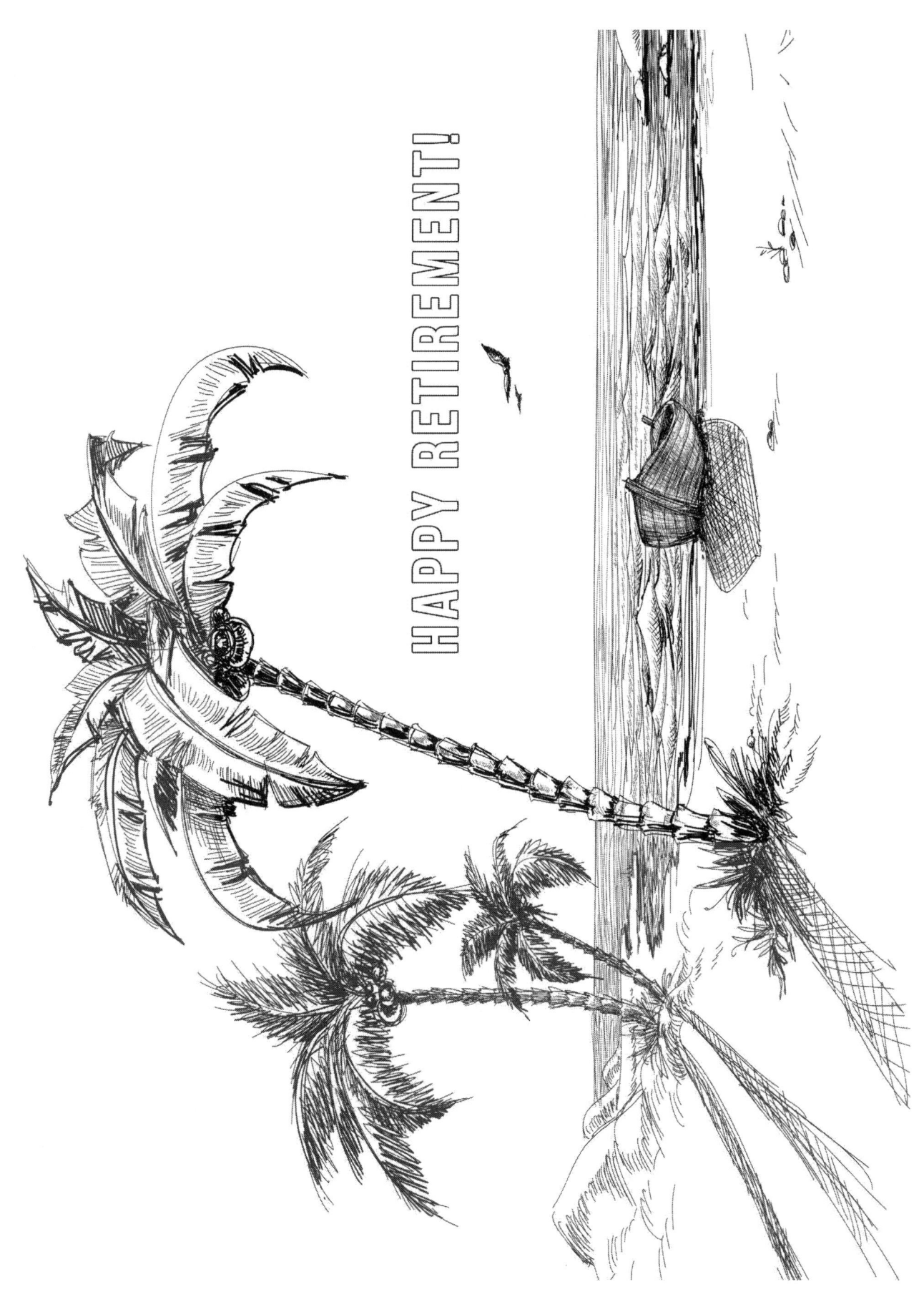

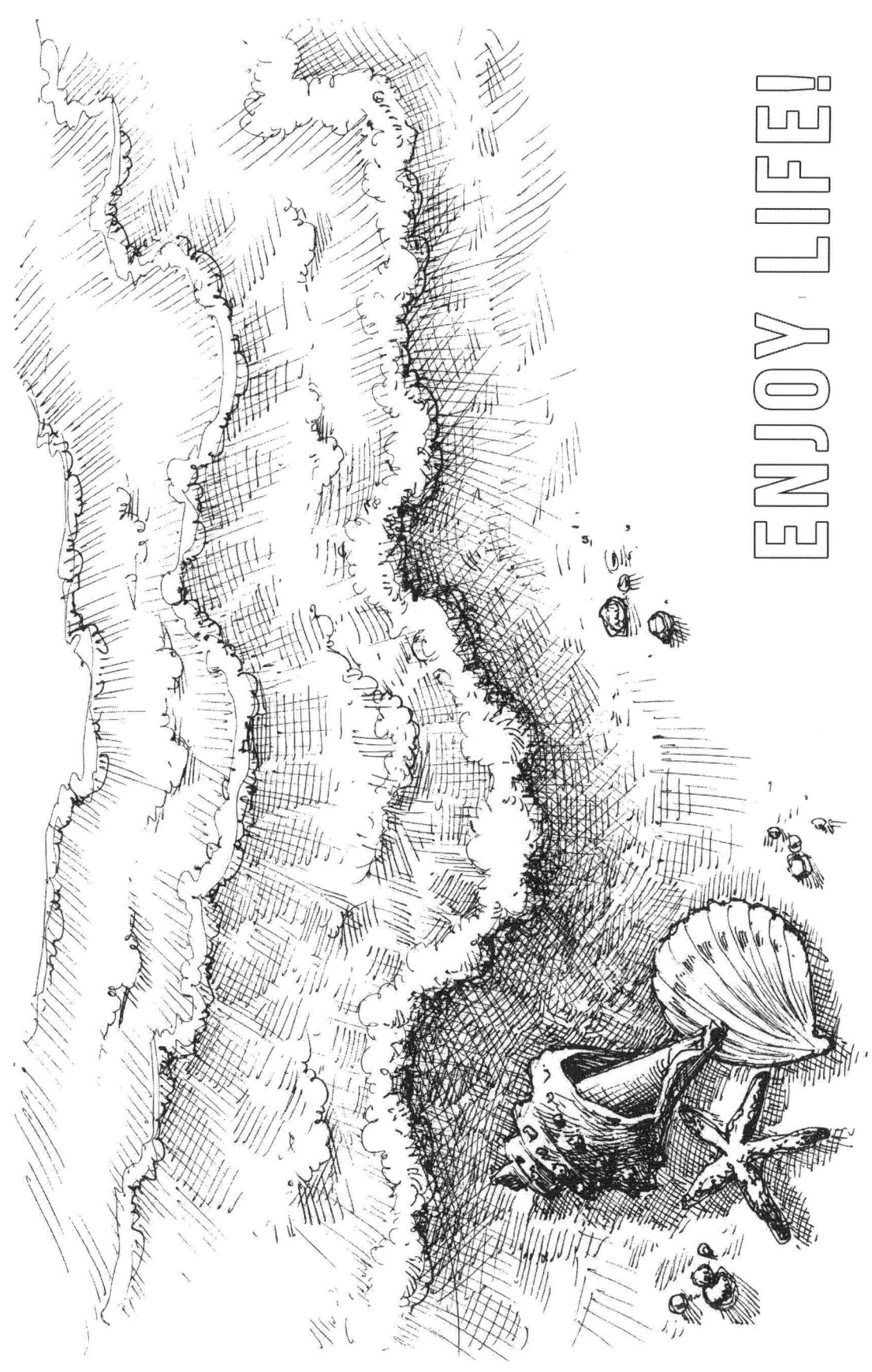

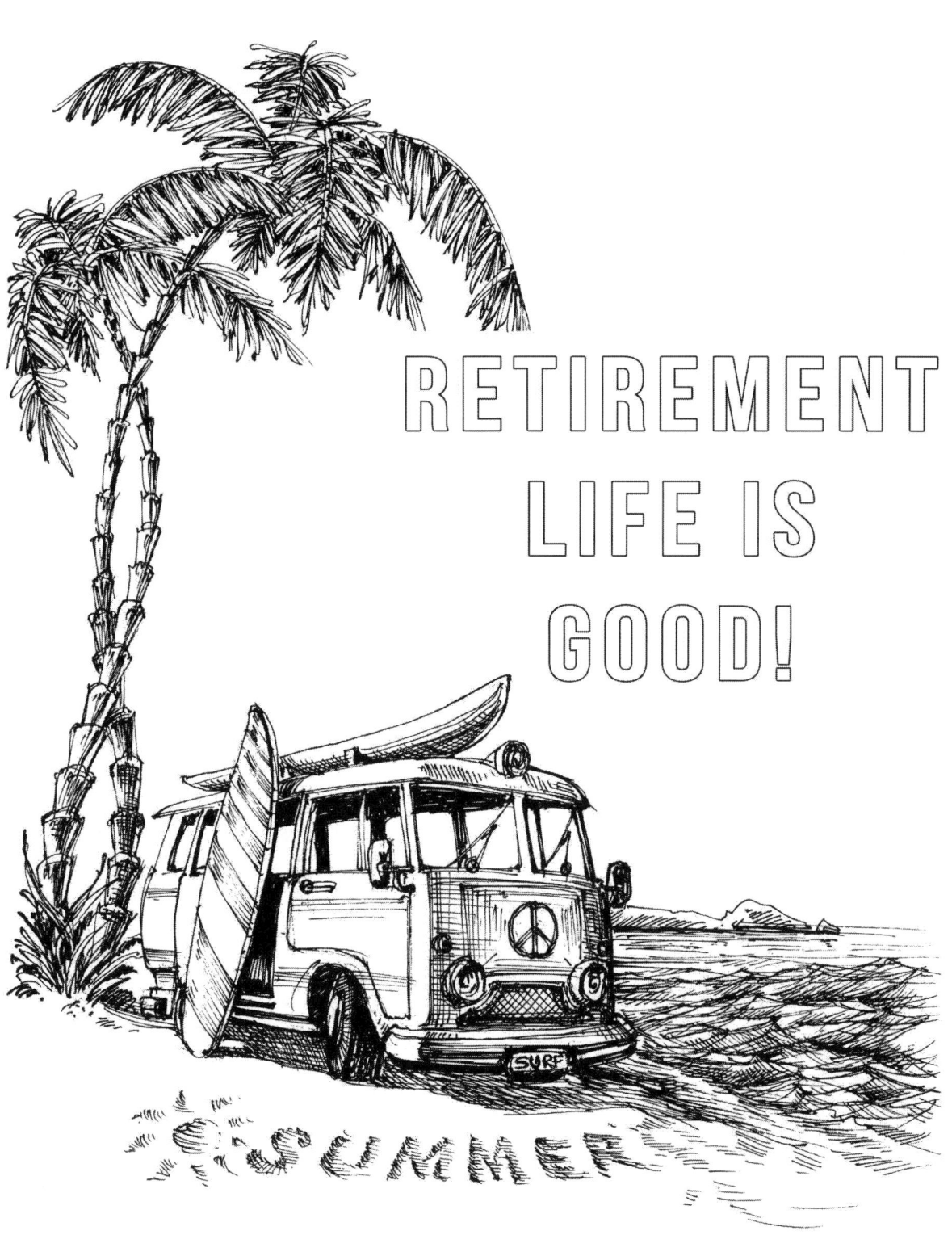

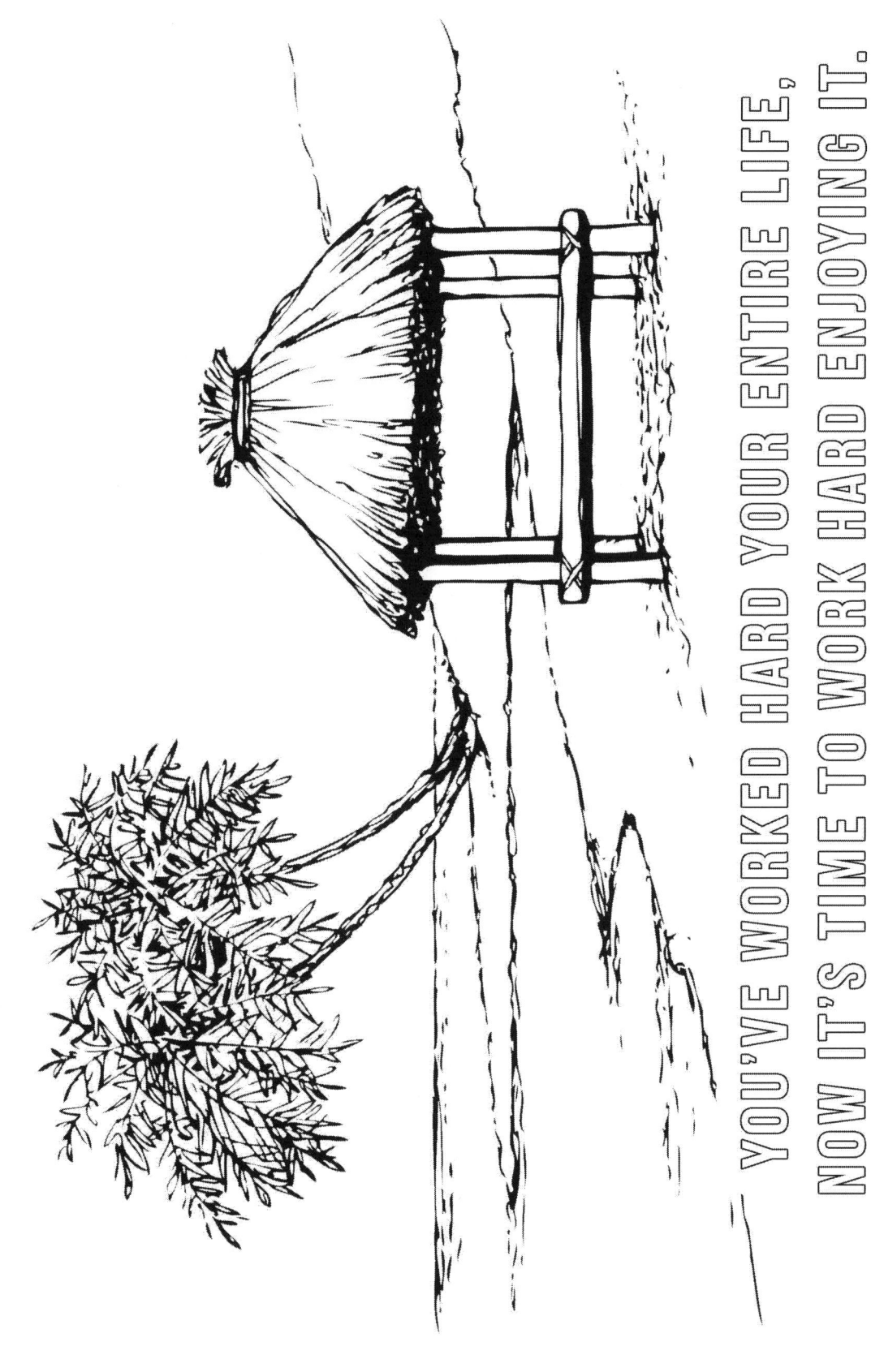

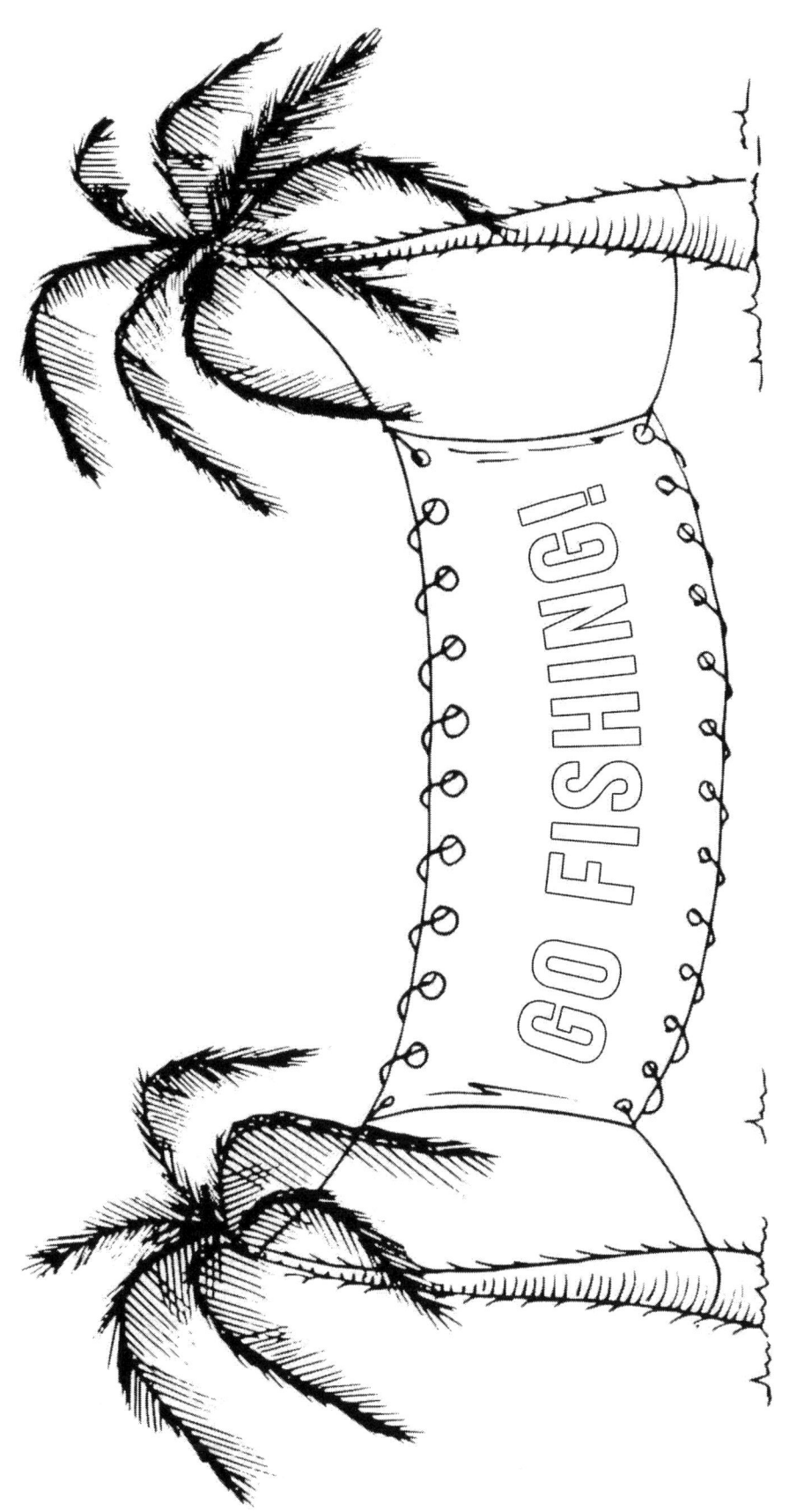

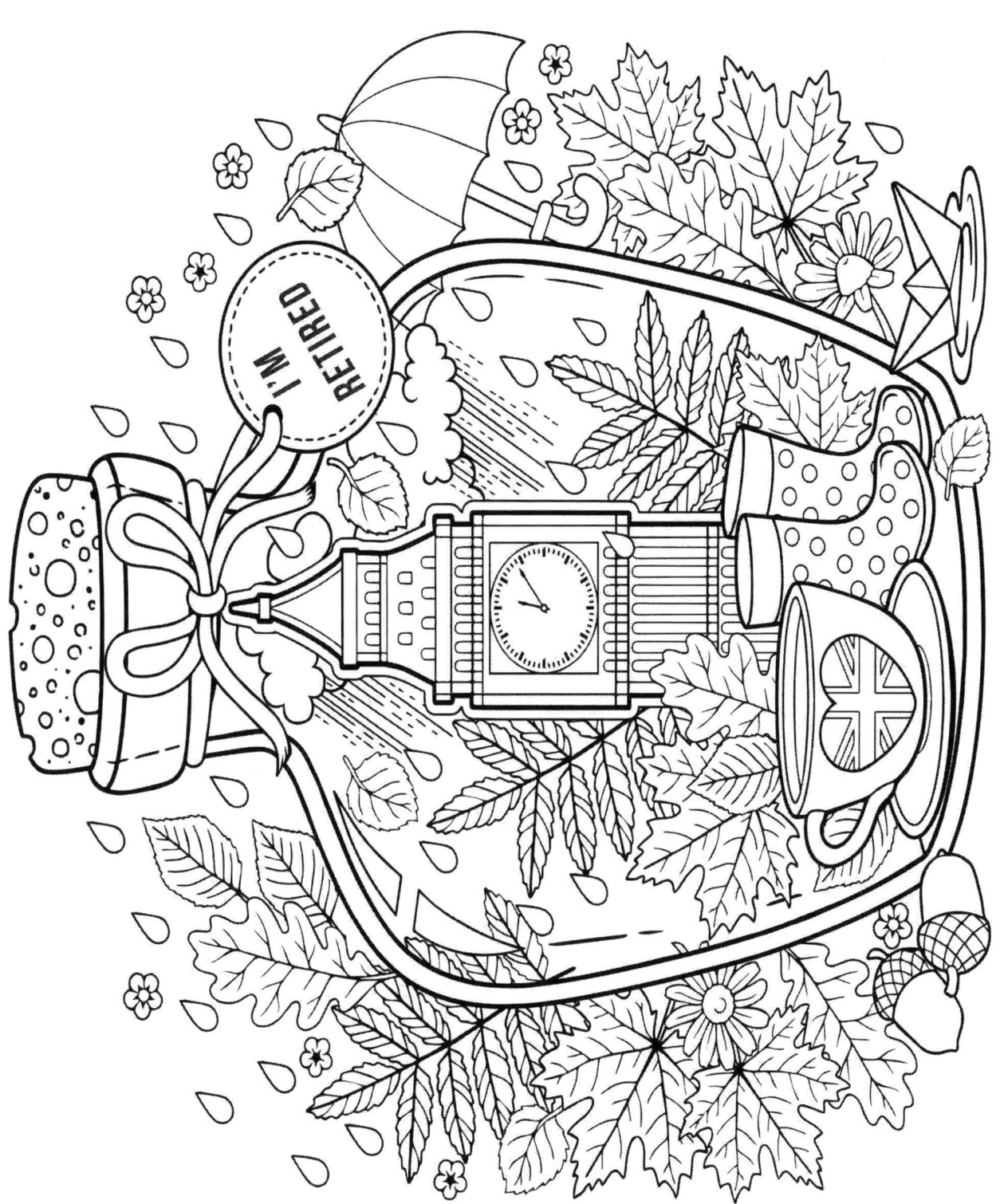

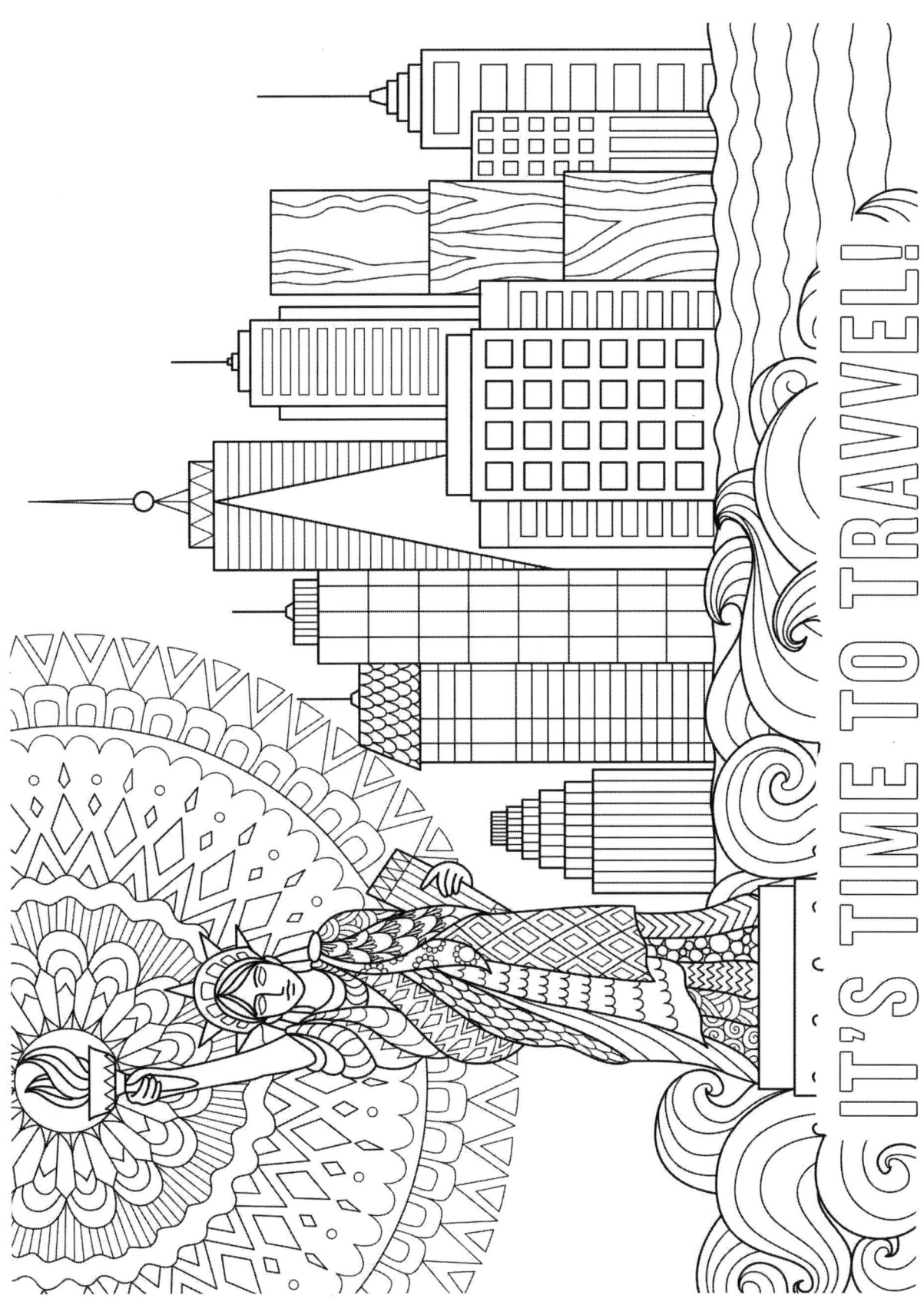

Made in the USA
Lexington, KY
12 June 2019